S0-BVT-839

NO LONGER PROPERTY OF
SEATTLE PUBLIC LIBRARY

RUNAWAY

ROAD

Goofy Guru Publishing presents . . .

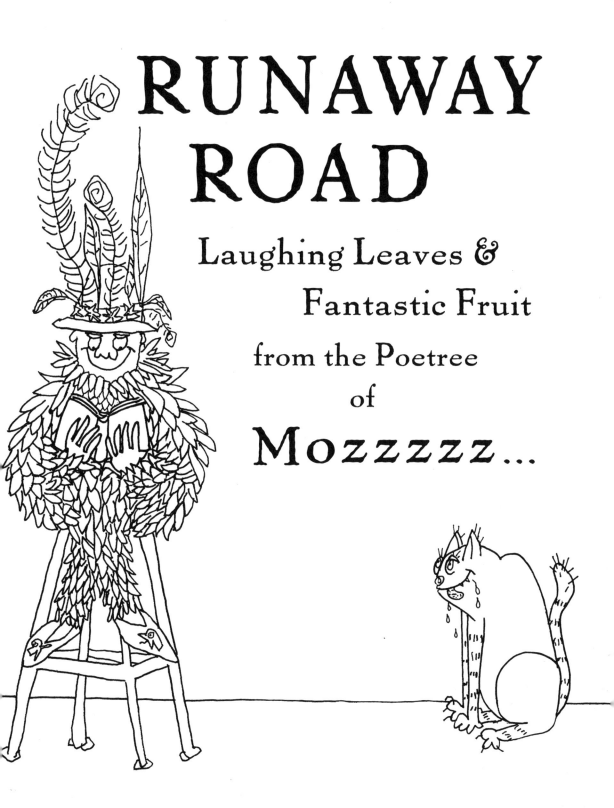

RUNAWAY ROAD

Laughing Leaves &
Fantastic Fruit
from the Poetree
of
Mozzzzz...

Copyright © 2004 by Chris Mosdell

All rights reserved. Neither this book nor any part thereof may be used or reproduced in any manner whatsoever without prior written permission from the publisher.

Goofy Guru Publishing
Alice "Apple" Apel, Editor-in-Chief
405 Kiowa Place, Boulder, CO 80303, USA
goofygurupress@comcast.net
www.goofyguru.com

Design by Jane Raese

Arigatoh-oh t' Lady Lyngo-go (mo ichi do),
a scroobious sniff f' the gift of E.L.'s nostrils,
a wee wink f' the three heads of Uncle Ed,
a paponic pogo f' Kid Nap f' balancing the Big Babble, &
a moo-cowkow t' ol' Mad Manji & his Immortal Mountain.

Library of Congress Control Number: 2004105381
ISBN 0-9726130-1-3

Printed in China.
First printing

This is a companion volume to
The Pearls of Wisdumb: The Electric Light Verse and Shocking Scribbles of Mozz.

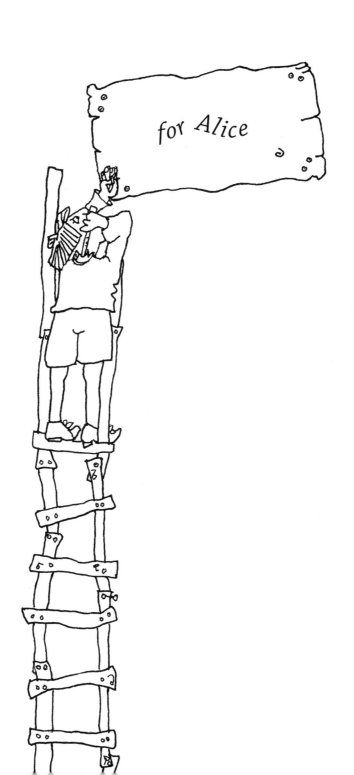

for Alice

THE TAILOR OF TALES

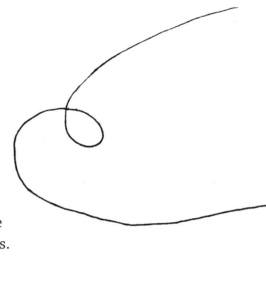

The Tailor of Tales is sewing
Fine silks of Once Upon a Time,
Sequined and braided in make-believe
From the remnants of nursery rhymes.
And with scissors and a busy needle
Darting with colored threads,
He is making outfits right off the peg
To be worn as if they were read.

Fashionable fables for one and all
In silver, gold, and sunset red—
Sleeves that shine in sleeping beauty
With collars of what an ogre said.
Pantaloons from magic spells,
See-through veils of a Long Time Ago,
Great big buttons of witches' warts,
And Happily-Ever-After robes.

And so he sits and steadily sews
Stars on a darkened velvet night,
Stitching the moon upon a satin shirt
Where Good and Evil fight.
A cloak for a king all covered
In four and twenty blackbirds,
And a jacket designed from the invisible,
From words that are still unheard.

Still, the Tailor of Tales will sew
A story especially for you
That will fit like a prince's glove
Over adventures old and new.
And when you slip it on,
It will be as light as air,
Snipped and sewn with infinite care,
A tale now ready to wear.

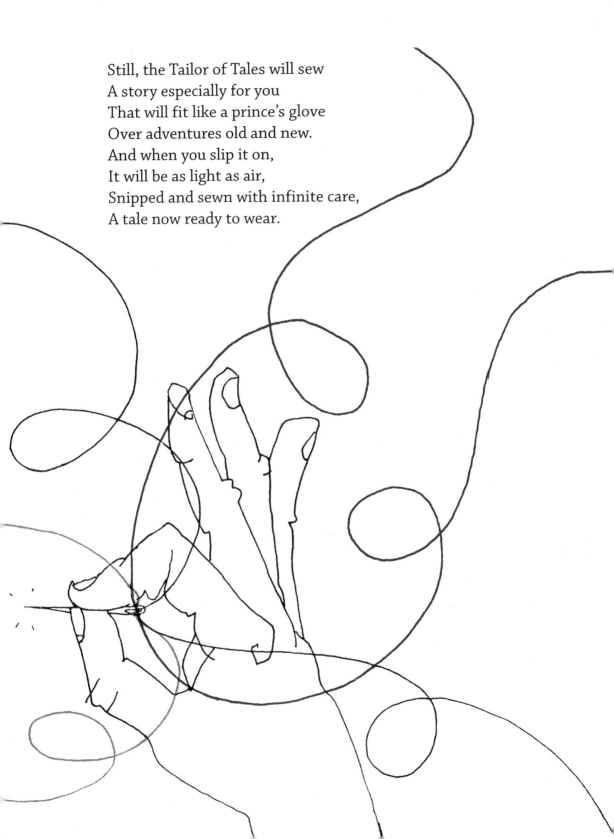

AN UNLOCKED LIFE

I found the Key to Life as it lay
On the garden path the other day,
But no lock would it unlock—
No door, no chest, no box.
And though you might
Be rather shocked
(Maybe or maybe not),
As that extraordinary key
Had no use for me—
Well, on that fateful day
I simply threw it away,
And into the great wide Goofy Garden
Off I went to play . . .

THIS WAY . . . THIS WAY . . .

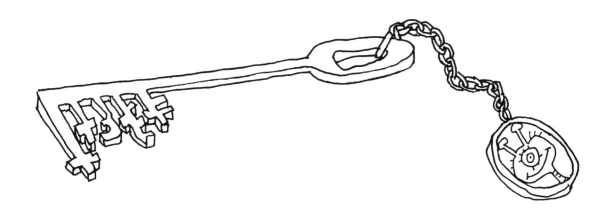

IN THE BEGINNING
THERE WAS A BOWL

Some say everything started out
As a great big bowl of primeval soup,
A gurgling and bubbling brew,
A steamy sludgy stew.
And that out of this great gooey mess,
As a kind of little test, the Almighty Creator
(Who knows soup comes first and dessert much later)
Then gave birth to everything on Earth.
Seas, trees, centipedes,
Snails, whales, bats and birds,
And the myriad of miracles of this wondrous world.

So if I'm to believe all that I've heard,
And that that was just a little test,
Then I'm very, very impressed—
Wow, Almighty Creator, you're the best!
(A million times better at your tests than I am at mine, I guess!)
But some things never change, I must confess,
'Cause as for that primeval soup
And that primeval stew, too,
We still have them served at school.
But now they're made by another "almighty"—
An almighty fool!

FIRST THINGS FIRST

I wasn't the first to observe
That water is decidedly wet.
I wasn't the first to surmise
That the sun rises before it sets.
I wasn't the first to realize
The Earth is round, not flat,
But I was the first to wear
A teapot for a flowered hat.

I wasn't the first to know
That toes usually occur in rows.
I wasn't the first to remark
That some worms even glow.
I wasn't the first to notice
A piggy's tail tends to curl,
But I was the first to take
A bath in a Chinese urn.

I wasn't the first to perceive
The sky's above,
    not below, the ground.
I wasn't the first to fathom
That a circle is always round.
I wasn't the first to recognize
That fish fingers never
    have hands,
But I was the first to eat
A sandwich made from sand.

I wasn't the first to notice
That hippopotami seldom fly.
I wasn't the first to understand
That islands really don't have eyes.
I wasn't the first to suggest
That a seesaw can't saw the sea,
But I was the first to play
The piano with my knees.

And the first to sleep
On a bed of snails,
And the first to teach
A school of whales.
And the first to pirouette
Upon my nose,
And the first to juggle
With toads, I suppose.

Oh but I'm not a great adventurer
Nor a mighty conquistador.
I wasn't the first to navigate
My way to unknown shores.
Still, I do take pride for sure,
Though it's not for fame I thirst,
But I truly can take credit
For the things that I did first.

THE MORNING OF THE AFTERNOON

T'is the morning of the afternoon,
A most pleasant time of year
To juggle jugs and china mugs
And clean out grubby ears.
To turn the house all inside out
And back to front at last,
To go and gargle with soapy suds
And throw out all the past.

T'is the morning of the afternoon,
And it's come before too soon.
A time to take down curtain ruffs
And exchange the forks for spoons,
To dust beneath the armpits,
To frolic and to sing,
To wear fur muffs as trouser cuffs
And forget important things.

T'is the morning of the afternoon,
And all across this ageless earth
They're pulling off their bedroom sheets
And wearing them as shirts.
They're rolling up the flowered carpets
And cavorting across the floor,
Taking out their back front teeth
And eating jelly raw.

Oh it's the morning of the afternoon,
A most pleasant time of year
To juggle jugs and china mugs
And clean out grubby ears.

THE YAWN CHORUS

I've seen them yawning
In the morning,
All gaping,
Gobby and wide.
Some say it's early exercise,
Some say it's when they smile.

I've seen them yawning
When it's dawning,
All sleepy and
Deeply snuggulous.
I've seen them as they jumble and rush,
I've seen them on the bus.

I've seen them yawning
And I've given them warnings,
But they take no notice of what they're told.
For they open wide
Like caves' insides,
And swallow themselves up whole.

THE DAY THE MOON FELL IN THE SEA
(For dear ol' Edward Lear)

The day the moon fell in the sea,
The silvery shoals of herring,
Of hurrying halibut,
All turned to gold
(Or so I'm told)
As far as the eye could see.

The day the sun fell in the sea,
The little octopi
Got hot beneath the collar
And puffed up and perspired
As if they were on fire
Or soaking in a pot of tea.

The day the stars fell in the sea,
The ancient periwinkles
Within the water weeds
Lost their wrinkles
And began to twinkle
Like the last of a luminous breed.

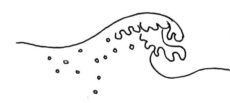

And the golden halibuttery,
The periwinkley twinkly,
The puffed-up and peculiar breed
Looked up at the sky above
And said, "I think that's about enough
Of things that go plop
And unexpectedly drop
Into the silliness we call our sea."

RUNAWAY ROAD

Didn't I say, today's the day,
Today's the day we're gonna run away?
Down to the bottom of Runaway Road,
Across the fields into the Great Unknown.
Under a carefree cloudless sky
With never a tear in our twinkling eyes,
Never a sigh or a backward glance,
Just a gypsy jig and a hobo dance,
As we run, run, run down Runaway Road,
Running away to never come home.

And we'll pack our knapsacks on our backs
With gold and emeralds and treasures that
We'll find all scattered on our bedroom floors.
Heirlooms we can trade in for pennies on a far-off shore,
Where we'll pass by the palaces of real royalty
And be invited in for snootwiches and tea.
But of course we won't stop, 'cause we're like the wind—
We can never be captured nor caged in
As we run, run, run down Runaway Road,
Running away to never come home.

And we'll sing our songs of freedom and fun
Under the eye of a jolly ol' sun,
And we'll follow the stars like birds fly south,
Forgetting all about our silly ol' house.
And we'll converse with those who have also traveled,
And all the mysteries of life will unravel.
And we'll do what we want at any ol' time,
And the world will be ours—just yours and mine,
As we run, run, run down Runaway Road,
Running away to never come home.

And we'll eat wild berries and drink from the streams,
And life will be perfect, as if it's a dream.
And we'll sniff the fresh air, and we'll go, "Oh yummy!
Smells like home cooking or so say our tummies."
And we'll forget about freedom and life on our own
And snootwiches 'n' tea and the royals on their thrones.
And the thrills and the spills of the Great Unknown,
And the seeds of adventures we were about to sow,
And we'll run, run back down Runaway Road,
'Cause it'll be time for dinner in our silly ol' home.

Are you sure it was today we were gonna run away?
How about tomorrow? What d' y' say?

WHAT MISTER KNOW-IT-ALL DIDN'T KNOW

Mister Know-It-All has changed his name,
For only the other day
I asked Mister Know-It-All,
"Are you really sure you know it all?"
And he looked at me with that know-it-all look,
With that I've-read-every-single-book look,
And said, "There is nothing I do not know."
So I go, "Where does the scent of a rose go
After it goes up your nose?"
And he sniffed and sniffed, and again he sniffed,
And said, "Ah, I wish . . . I wish . . .
But I do not know the answer to this!"
So maybe I'm the one to blame
For Mister Know-It-All changing his name.

THE SPAGHETTI YETI

I've never meti
Anyone yeti
Who's seen
The Spaghetti Yeti.
(Or ever had one for a peti.)
But they say to geti
This rare yeti,
Place a plate of spaghetti
Under a neti
Just about sunseti.

Though somehow I beti
You'll never seti
Eyes on this allusive yeti.
Still, don't fretti—
You can always forgeti
About the yeti.
Pack up the neti,
Watch the sunseti,
And tuck into that spaghetti!

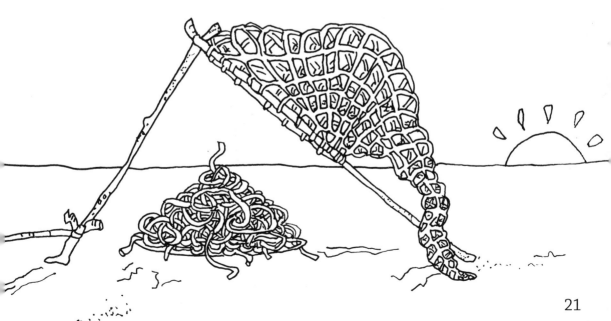

HIGH-CLASS SOCIETY

Unlike you and me,
The members of the Stilt Society

Think themselves very superior and elite.

A cut above us all, for sure—

Sticking their noses in the air
As they walk on down the street.

Snootily striding past
On their tall spindly masts,

Believing they're the last
Of an extremely high class.

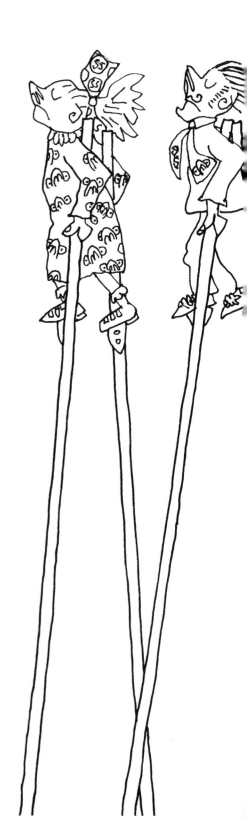

YOGA OGRES

Perhaps if ogres
Practiced yoga
Their days as ogres
Would be over.

For if they just said, "OM,"
Instead of "UGH!"
Maybe they wouldn't be
Such unbearable thugs,

But blissfully happy,
Like pigs in clover,
When the sun comes out
In mid-October.

IRON ON THE LOOSE

Iron! Iron! Iron!
No, not lion, *IRON*!

There's an iron on the loose—
A flat-faced ferocious steaming brute!

But don't worry,
From experience I've learnt
That if it leaps on you, you won't get hurt.

At the very worst,
You'll have a freshly pressed skirt or shirt.

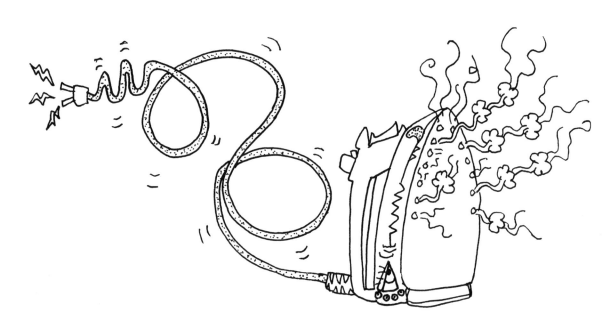

FRIENDS I'D LOVE TO MEET AGAIN

I used to have a friend called Victor
Who taught etiquette to boa constrictors.
"Now say, 'Please'
Before you squeeze."
But long time, no see, indeed.

I used to have a friend called Samantha
Who brushed the coats of panthers.
Kept them smooth,
And glossy too,
But where, oh where, are you?

I used to have a friend called Miles
Who sympathized with crocodiles.
He'd soothe their fears,
Dry their tears,
But I haven't seen him for years.

I used to have a friend called Rita
Who counted the spots on cheetahs.
A mathematician courageous,
Notating numbers onto pages,
But I haven't seen her for ages.

Oh friends, I'd love to meet you all again,
But who knows where, knows when?

I'd love to meet you all again,

Before dear friends, my long-lost friends,
You come to sticky ends.

THE SILLY FLYING GOLDFISH SONG

I saw five goldfish flying—
Oh to be them
I wished!
The sun it was
A gilded dish—
What a perfect day for fish.

I saw four goldfish flying
In a sky
Of runny honey.
They must have been
All gummy
From their tails down to their tummies.

I saw three goldfish flying
Above that
Mountain range—
They looked like
Orange aeroplanes
But not so unduly strange.

I saw two goldfish flying,
Fluttering
Through the air.
I had to stop
And stand and stare,
For nothing did they wear.

I saw a goldfish flying—
It sang
This silly song,
A little shorter
Than it was long,
But now it's come and gone.

Oh I saw five goldfish flying,
As if it were
A dream—
The clouds all made
Of freshly whipped cream . . .
A lovely scene, indeed.

A lovely scene, indeed.

27

BLINKING AND WINKING
AT THE GREAT EYE BALL

Oh what a spectacle for all,
The night of the Great Eye Ball.
The blinking and the winking were there,
Those who gazed or simply stared.
Those who fluttered their lovely long lashes,
The shortsighted and those in dark glasses.
Those who squinted and those who twinkled,
The young and the old and the wrinkled.
Those made up with mascara on thick,
Those in monocles and a bit miasmic.
Oh the greens, and the browns, and the blues!
They all danced together in twos
Doing the Big Blurred Vision and the Cross-Eyed Joe,
Eye to eye, not nose to nose.
Beautifully beady all through the night,
Savoring all the senses of sight,
Until drowsy and droopy,
Lids as heavy as lead,
They did the Shut Eye
And went off to bed.

MY DAD, THE DULT

My father keeps promising
He'll tell me lots of things
When I become a dult.
A dult?
What's a dult?
Dult! Dult?
I've looked it up
And the word just doesn't exist.
Umm . . . I think my dad's losing it.
For he's not as young as he used to be.
Now he's imagining things like dults
When he goes and talks to me!
Huh, if anyone's a dult, it's him for sure.
But what do I want to become one for?
He must think I'm mad.
Who'd wanna be a dult like my dad?

THE MOON DUNE BLOOM
AND THE RINGED RACCOON

Let's shed a silent tear
For the moon dune flower
That blooms only once
Every ten-thousand years
At exactly the same hour.

And on that very day
Along comes a ringed raccoon
(The one with the floppy ears)
That only eats a moon dune bloom
Once every ten-thousand years.

And then precisely at noon
It goes and eats that bloom—
Ah, is this a prediction of doom?
Will the world end soon?
Is it some cosmic sign
That we're all running out of time?
Or is it just that a hungry raccoon
Only thinks of eating a moon dune bloom
Once every ten-thousand years?
(They say it's good for floppy ears)

Ah, if only we knew! If only we knew!
Is it doom or just a delicious bloom?
Coincidence or the hand of fate?
A prophecy or a yummy taste?

Ah, if only we knew! If only we knew!
Still, let's pity the poor moon dune
And shed a silent tear.
(Well, at least once every ten-thousand years.)

THE UNLUCKY LETTUCE

Said the rabbit,
"Little lettuce leaf,

If I nibble your ear
Will you weep?

If I nibble your nose
With my little teeth

Or nibble your fingers,
Will you go 'EEK'?

Oh tell me, tell me please—
If so, little you, I won't eat."

But the little lettuce leaf
Didn't seem to speak,

Though secretly it beseeched
With high-pitched supersonic
squeaks

That, of course, the rabbit
didn't hear.

"Huh, a bunny with cloth ears!"
Shrieked the lettuce.
"Just my luck!"
As it was quickly nibbled up.

PUMPKIN BOY IS BLUE

Poor Pumpkin Boy is blue
'Cause unlike me and you
He's never learnt to whistle—
Not even just a little,
And that's one thing he'll never do.

So behind those twinkling triangular eyes
And that big wide pumpkin smile, he cries,
"Boo-hoo! Boo-hoo! Boo-hoo!"
Oh Pumpkin Boy is blue,
For all he wants to do
Is simply purse his lips together
(Of course he knows that's never)
And whistle a little pumpkiny tune,
Just like me and you.

So beneath that orange halloweeny hue,
Poor ol' Pumpkin Boy is really blue—
Boo-hoo! Boo-hoo! Boo-hoo!
But what is a pumpkin to do?

33

TIGHTROPE OF TERROR

A rope of knotted snakes,
One wrong step to seal his fate,
Though t'was not for walking barefoot
   along that venomous line,
But a sight that chilled his blood,
That caused his sad demise.

THE SONG OF THE GOBBLING GOBLINS

The Gobbling Goblins are terribly toothless,
Their gobs great grotesque and rubbery ol' things
That slobber unduly and drool so rudely
With bits from the bins within.

The Gobbling Goblins are Neanderthal nasty,
And their hands are all glutinous and grim,
And soupy and sickly and slimy
From grabbing up garbage and shoveling it in.

And they come just after the sun has set,
Grasping and groping with their giant nets,
And as they come they sing this song
(And if you want you can sing along):

We're gonna
Gobble up, gobble up,
Gobble up the world.
Gobble up, gobble up,
Every boy 'n' every girl.
F' Gobbling Goblins indeed we are,
We're gonna gobble up the earth
'N' the moon 'n' the stars.
'N' when we've gobbled
Till everything's gone,
We're gonna gobble 'n' gobble
'N' gobble up this song!

Oh the Gobbling Goblins are crude and uncouth,
And their faces are mucousy and messy and gross,
All stuck up with yuck like mushy manure,
Runny egg 'n' dregs 'n' dried-on toast.

And they come with their tongues all sticking out,
All drippy 'n' frothy 'n' coated in goo,
And they slobber as they sing their slimy old song,
As they gobble along on the lookout for you:

We're gonna
Gobble up, gobble up,
Gobble up the world.
Gobble up, gobble up,
Every boy 'n' every girl.
F' Gobbling Goblins indeed we are.
We're gonna gobble up the earth
'N' the moon 'n' the stars.
'N' when we've gobbled
Till everything's gone
We're gonna gobble 'n' gobble
'N' gobble up this song!

Oh listen! Oh listen!
It's the Gobbling Song—

Listen, but be careful,

Don't listen long.

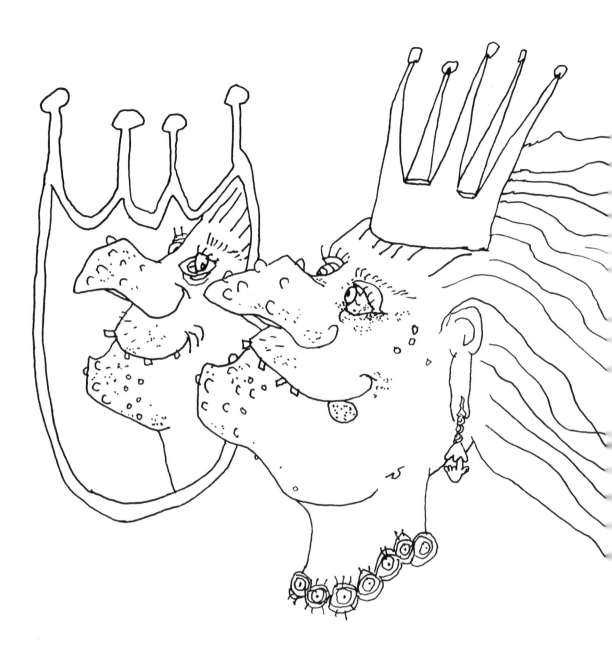

WHAT A QUEEN CAN SEE

"Mirror, mirror on the wall,
You don't have to tell me anything at all.

"You don't have to tell me
That I'm spottier than Snow White,
That I'm tardier than Cinderella,
That I've more warts than the Wicked Witch,
That I'm ruder than Rumplestiltskin,
That I'm more pompous than the Handsome Prince,
That I'm uglier than the Ugly Duckling,
That I'm redder than Little Red Ridinghood,
Or that I'm hairier than the Big Bad Wolf.

"In fact, as I can see,
I'm obviously the best, the utmost—
Absolutely supreme," said the queen,
Looking into the mirror with a smile quite serene.

"Umm . . . ," thought the mirror,
"It's nothing to do with me,"

And smiled back silently.

GOONY GANG

Cross-eyed goony gulls
Are really hooligulls

That screech
Along the beach,

Not caring in the least
'Bout those who walk beneath.

MAN FROM JAPAN

There was a young man from Japan,
Whose face was an expandable fan,
So when it was hot, people liked him a lot,
That very cool man from Japan.

FIENDSHIP 'N' FRIENDSHIP

Wolfboy Bill and Moonfaced Phil
Were always the best of friends,
But that friendship nearly came to an end
When . . .

Bill kept howling at poor ol' Phil
(It really made him feel quite ill).
Still . . .

What are friends for,
If the little things they can't ignore?

UNCLE ED (WHO LOST HIS HEAD)

Uncle Ed lost his head
Somewhere between breakfast and bed.
Did he leave it on the bathroom floor?
Did it roll behind the living-room door?
Well, we've all looked and looked and looked some more,
'Cause it's difficult to ignore
Uncle Ed without his head.
(And it must be said
That for Uncle Ed
It's inconvenient, for sure.)
For he'd love to scratch it
And think, "Now where did I leave my head?"
But I'm afraid, well, he's having to scratch
Somewhere else instead.

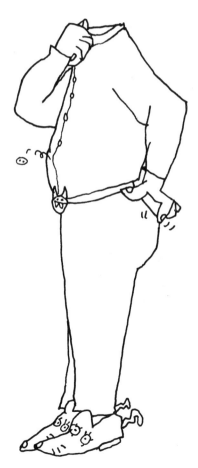

THE ROBIN HOOD OF MUSIC

He put the violin
To his chin,

Then took the bow
And let the violin go—

Like so . . .

Oh!

WARNING:
Shooting a violin
Can be a very dangerous thing,
But if this is what you intend to do,
Trust me, it'll soon be completely out of tune!

MERMAIDS AND WORM-PIE MEALS
(And the Moral Behind Wearing Masks)

When he wore his lobster mask
And stood beside the sea,
All the little mermaids sang,
"Come and stay for tea,
And swim amongst the seaweed,
Blow bubbles through your nose,
And live with us forever
Till east the west wind blows."

And when he wore his swallow mask
And stood in the open fields,
All the birdies sang to him,
"Come dine on worm-pie meals
And circle round the golden globe
While warbling through the blue,
And stay forever and a day
Till our songs are out of tune."

And when he wore his caterpillar mask
And stood beneath the trees,
Not a single song did he ever hear—
No calls to stay for tea.
Still, all those little birdies came
And on him they did feed,
And all the little mermaids sang,
"What a silly boy, indeed."

SMUG SLUGS

I hate slugs
Who are smug,
All slippery
And slimy
With complacent smiley mugs.

I hate slugs
Who lie like rugs,
All content
And cozy
As if they've just been hugged.

I can handle bugs,
But slugs?
Slippery, slimy,
Complacent smug slugs—
UGH!

SHOCKING SHOE NEWS

There once was an old woman who lived in a shoe.
She had so many children, she didn't know what to do . . .

Till the owner of the shoe came back.
And after that . . .

She still didn't know what to do,
'Cause she was, I'm afraid to say . . .

SHOE GOO!

(And her children too!)

OK! OK! Don't be blue.
It's not true. It's not true.
I just felt like shocking you.

(Still, be careful when putting on your shoes.)

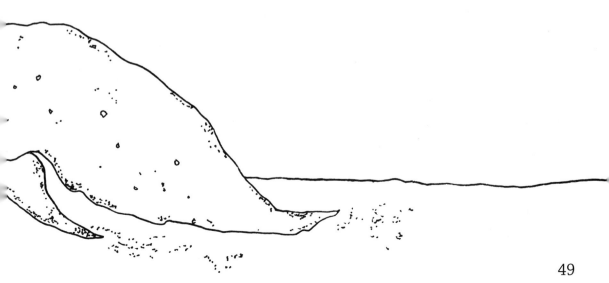

HOLEY! HOLEY! HOLEY!

Might I, might I be so bold
As to inquire, "What is a hole?"
I've had one in my pocket,
I've had one in my net,
But as to what one is,
I haven't fathomed yet.

I heard there was a holy man
Just south of Timbuktu,
But on meeting him I'm sad to say
There was nothing new he knew.

Most things can be divided,
Cut in two or three,
But I've never heard of half a hole—
Umm . . . mysterious indeed.

MOZZ
MEDITATING
MOZZ

ON WHAT
THE HECK
IS
A HOLE.

As if from out of nowhere,
A hole it just appears.
You can see right through it
(As if it wasn't there),
But it is, and that's what's weird.

You can't put your finger on one.
There's nothing there to feel.
If I were a wise philosopher
I'd wonder, "Oh what is real?"

But perhaps in some far-off day,
When I'm extremely old,
They'll come and ask, "Oh Uncle Mozz,
What really is a hole?"
And I'll rub my wizened chin
And say, "My dears, I've been
Up and down, and round and round,
And all the world I've strolled,
But still I'm in a quandary.
I've queried and I've quibbled,
And yet I've no idea
The answer to that riddle."

THE DANCER OF DANCES

I've danced The Electric Eel,
I've danced The Three-Legged Chair,
I've danced The Fairground Ferris Wheel,
I've danced The Lighter Than Air.
I've danced The Whirl and The Wiggle,
I've danced The Ten-Ton Whale,
I've danced The Tadpole Wriggle,
I've danced The Flapping Sails.
I've danced The Overheated Machine,
I've danced The Dying Swallow,
I've danced The Leapfrogging Queen,
I've danced The Muddy Wallow.
I've danced The High on the Hog,
I've danced The Runaway Train,
I've danced The Stuck in the Bog,
I've danced The Flickering Flame.
I've danced The Unearthly Emu,
I've danced The Fox and Hounds,
I've danced The Waves at Seaview.
Now to dance The All Fall Down . . .

Or perhaps The Collapse, The Knocked-Out Flat,
The Splat, or Where the Elephant Sat.

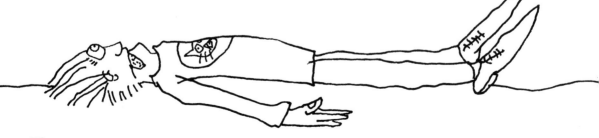

WHY WEEP, LITTLE WILLOW?

Why weep,
Little willow?

See, the grass is all soggy and soaked.

Is it because you were bitten
By that naughty gnarled old oak?

But dry your tears,
Little willow.

Everything will be all right.

The oak's an awful ogre,
But its bark is worse than its bite.

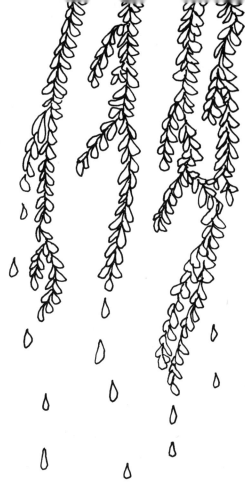

53

THE FEATHERED SUIT AND HAT
(A Short Poetry Play in Three Acts)

ACT ONE

He wore his feathered suit
Of royal budgie blue,
Parrot pink, and warbler green,
And shining hummingbird hues.
And on his head a feathered hat
Of flaming flamingo red,
A peacock's plume, an emu's too,
And an ostrich one to match.

ACT TWO

And there he serenely sat,
Elegantly eaglely, superiorly swanly,
Slightly turkey-fat.
A wonder of the world—
A magnificent human bird
In that suit of fantastic feathers
And that stupendous feathered hat.

AND NOW FOR THE FINAL ACT

(And this is a little sad;
Very sad, in fact . . .)

Yes, there he sat,
In his feathered suit and hat,

'Til along came a cat.
Then that was that—

A feathered suit and hat snack.

BYE-BYE, HUMAN FLY

Some might have envied the Human Fly.
Oh what a lucky guy
Flitting around above the ground,
Showing off swooping and wheeling
And landing up there on the ceiling.

Ah yes, lucky guy that Human Fly.
Well, that is until the time
He was flying around like so
And caught the eye (Oh no!)
Of ol' Terry Toad from down the road.

(Who wasn't envious one little bit
Though he has a liking for things that flit.)
Who just stuck out his sticky tongue
As our Human Fly flew by
And popped him smartly in his tum—
My, my, some lucky guy!

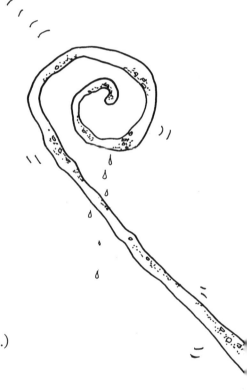

LITTLE LUCY LONG-LASHES

Little Lucy Long-Lashes,
Oh how she can fly—
All it takes is a couple of blinks,
And she sails into the sky.
One eye to turn her left;
One eye to turn her right;
Her nose, a little rudder;
Her ears to adjust the height.

She can hover like a hummingbird
By letting those long lashes flap.
She can lie mid-air upon her back.
(Though she's careful not to nap!)
And if you've ever met her,
In fact, I'll be very surprised,
For before you can say "Oh Lucy, hi!"
She's gone in the wink of an eye.

(And as for ol' Terry below,
Lucy's not worried a bit.
She's really far too quick
For that tubby toady twit.)

THE NEVER EVERS
(Don'ts of the animal kingdumb)

Never plead for a piece of apple python.
Never ever wear a snapping turtleneck.
Never shave with a razorback whale.
Never call a mobster lobster, "Hey shrimp!"
Never dress in red round a bellowing bullfrog.
Never try to open a toot-tooting toucan.
Never place your luggage on a railway raccoon.
Never lock your door with a misplaced monkey.
Never play cards with a devious cheetah.
Never dance the quickstep with an orangutango.
Never expect much of interest from a great big boar.
Never ever goose a traumatized chicken.
Never stamp your letters with a three-ton seal.
Never greet a hyena with, "Hi, Ena!"
Never trust your Steinway to a piano tuna.
Never ask a hummingbird to whistle a tune
Never make a peanut butter and jellyfish sandwich.
Never joke around with a piranha-ha-ha.
Never play baseball with a vampire bat.
Never make a deal with a dirty rat.

Never ever . . . well, I could go on,
For of course the list is extremely long.
Though it's experience that counts
   On the road of life,
So I'll leave it to you
To choose wrong from right.

PIGGYBANKER

When I grow up I'm going to open
A piggybank, but on a really big scale.

Offering people to put their pennies
In my piggy—the size of a whale!

Oh, money will be safe with me,
For of course, I'll have the key

On a chain around my neck
('Cause I'll be president elect).

So for all you future investors,
Tomorrow's tycoons,

Get out your pennies.

I'm ready to collect.

NOT DRAWN TO SCALE

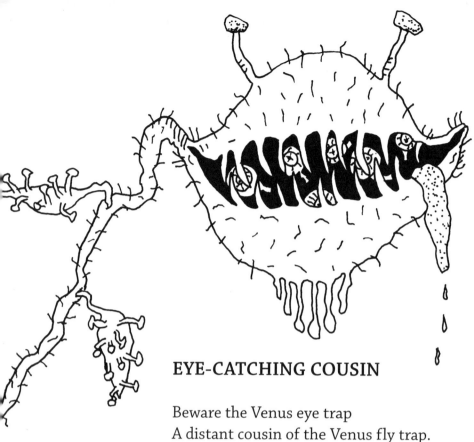

EYE-CATCHING COUSIN

Beware the Venus eye trap
A distant cousin of the Venus fly trap.

And trust my advice: keep well away—
Several hundred yards, I'd say.
For any closer than that,
Well, it's simply a matter of . . .

SNAP!

As an example, tragic indeed:
Perhaps the Venusians you've never seen,
Though they're known for their catlike curiosity,
With waving tentacles of a colossal size
But hey, surprise . . .

No eyes!

OLIVER TWIT
(The Boy Who Asked for Less)

Of course there's Oliver Twist,
The boy who asked for more.
I'm not like him at all—
I'm the boy who asked for less:
Less homework, fewer tests,
Less of everything I detest.

And the Chief of Terrible Tests and Horrible Homework
Towered over my head
And smiled a great big smile and said,
"Less homework? Fewer tests?
Why, of course, yes!"

But then his eyes glowed red,
And he laughed and laughed,
And his ears looked as if
    they were somehow smoking.
And he leered and looked down at me again
    and sneered,
"SORRY BOY, JUST JOKING!"

A BAA, BAA, BAA, AMONGST THE STARS
(Adventures of the Fantastic Flying Fleece)

A leap-about lamb,
  how sheepish I am
(Especially if you stare).
Leaping high
So all can spy
My wooly underwear.

A liftoff lamb, so frisky I am!
Farewell to fields and town.
Oh, hear me bleat
"The Flying Fleece"
Miles above the ground.

A look-around lamb,
  how buoyant I am
(And onward I am bound).

A cosmic cloud
Who will astound
By never coming down.

A leisurely lamb, afloat I am
Who sails the infinite blue.
A baa, baa, baa
Amongst the stars,
Up here, see me cruise.

A lunar lamb, Ewe.F.O. I am
(Yoo-hoo! I'll be landing soon).
Where I will graze
Far, far away
On the meadows of the moon.

NEXT TO NOTHING TIM

Next to Nothing Tim
Believes it's really a sin
That when the sun is out
One shouldn't be at home within.
But the question always begins
With "Why wear nothing, Tim?
Is that a natural thing?"
"But truly my clothes I'm in," says Tim.
"It's just I like to have them on
Not over, but under, my skin."

(But they still arrested him!)

ACTS OF ABSURDITY

The Python Impersonator
Bit himself
By mistake.
And so later
(For his health's sake),
He became a
Garden Rake Impersonator.

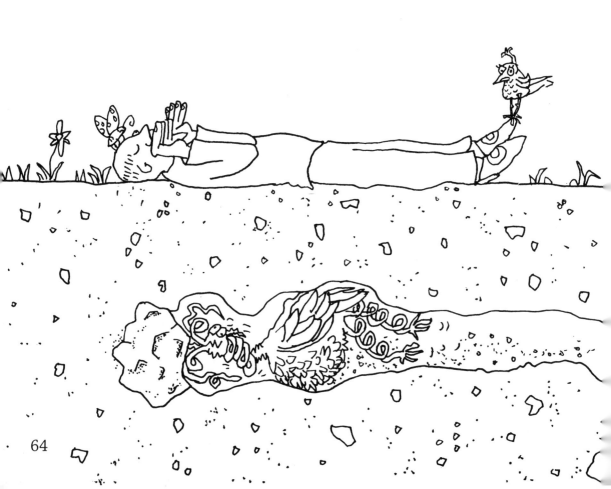

FEATHERS BENEATH YOUR FEET

The molebird's there beneath the turf,
Burrowing miles into the Earth,
Living almost exclusively
On beakfuls of grit and dirt.

It tunnels diligently underground,
Often in formation, in flocks,
Reaching the speed of twenty knots—
That is, till it hits a rock!

Somewhat like a feathered corkscrew,
Down and down and down it bores
To lay its eggs (and keep them warm)
At the Earth's far fiery core.

And though it's very rarely seen,
That muffled sound beneath your feet
Is probably a solitary song from the deep,
The molebird's "Tweet! Tweet! Tweet!"

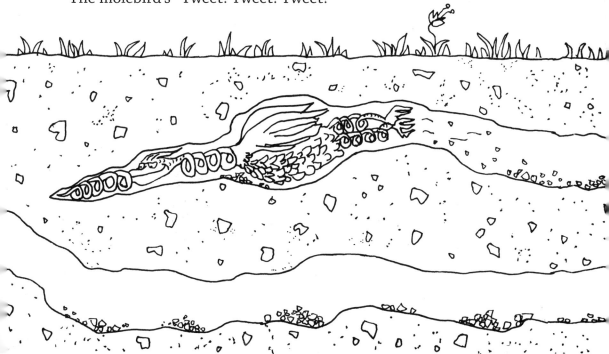

THE SCARY SNOW STORY

The Abominable Snowman
Came down the road,
Three hundred feet
Of towering, f-f-freezing snow,
Coal-black evil eyes
And a stiletto carrot nose—
Oh no! Oh no! Oh no!

The Abominable Snowman
Came down the road
Looking for me to eat
(Someone said I'd stolen his feet).
Came down the road
To bury me in snow—
Oh no! Oh no! Oh no!

And there I was upon the road . . .
Oh no! Oh no! Oh no!

And the Abominable Snowman towered over me so . . .
Oh no! Oh no! Oh no!

And I shivered there in his shadow . . .
Oh no! Oh no! Oh no!

And the world was dark and cold . . .
Oh no! Oh no! Oh no!

And I gave a little scary shout . . .
Oh no! Oh no! Oh no!

And the Abominable Snowman was just about . . .
Oh no! Oh no! Oh no!

When all at once the sun came out!
Oh yes! Oh yes! Oh yes!

What an awful gooey mess!

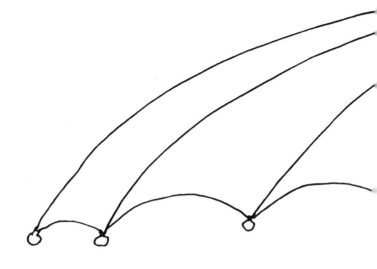

THE ORIGINAL IDEA

When first asked
To build an ark
And collect two of every animal
From leopards to larks,
Armadillos to aardvarks,
'Cause it was going to rain
Worse than on the plains of Spain,
Noah, being a clever fella,
Scratched his head
And suggested instead, "Well, er . . .
How about if I just go out
And buy an extra-big umbrella?"

MUSICAL MUTT

I gave my dog
An old trombone.
"Play some cool cat jazz," I said.
He barked "I only play the harp,"
And buried it instead.

"My dog thinks he's
A golden trumpet,"
I told the perplexed vet.
So like a thorn,
He took out the trum,
And (though he still plays the drums),
He's back to being a pet.

69

VANILLA GORILLA

The female vanilla gorilla
(That's the color, not the flavor),
A colossal creamy hairy pillar,
Exhibits the most enterprising behavior
Of exuding a musk called Jungle Killer.
So all the males, once acting like drunken sailors,
Are completely knocked out by such an anti-thriller
That comes from this natural distiller.
Indeed, the stuff's a true and tested gorilla tamer,
So you undoubtedly can't blame her
For using the ol' Jungle Killer—
An out 'n' out winner, a real vanilla gorilla chiller.

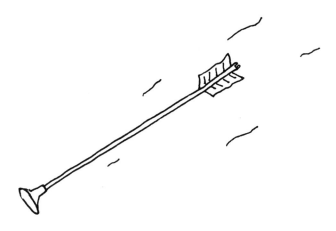

CROSS-EYED CUPID

Oh Cupid, shoot your arrow,
Shoot it nice and straight . . .

Er, OK . . .

Shall I blame your aim,
Or should I accept my fate?

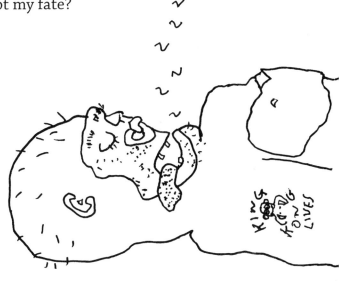

FIN FASHION

For creatures half aquatic
Like the fabulous flying fish
That wishes to remain in motion
Not below but above the ocean,
I present the over-water snorkel—
Perfect for this salty sparrow
While it glides across the water
Like a gulping scaly arrow.

THE SEA THAT STOPPED

With a single hand, I can stop the tide,
Right in front of your very eyes.
I can stop the sea—
Not an ebb, not a flow.
Right. Here goes.
Just watch me.
I just put up my hand like this
And say, "LISTEN TO ME! STOP, SEA!
And you see . . .
Did you watch? It stopped!
Well, just for a second, don't you reckon?

THE POPPING PRAYER

Oh God of Bubble Gum,
Be a chum—
Blow me a bubble
The size of the sun.

Oh God of Bubble Gum,
Be a friend—
Blow me a bubble
That will never end.

Oh God of Bubble Gum,
Almighty You—
Blow my friends bubbles,
And big ones, too!

Oh God of Bubble Gum,
Blow me another one . . .
But do this first—
Make all those other bubbles
Go and burst.

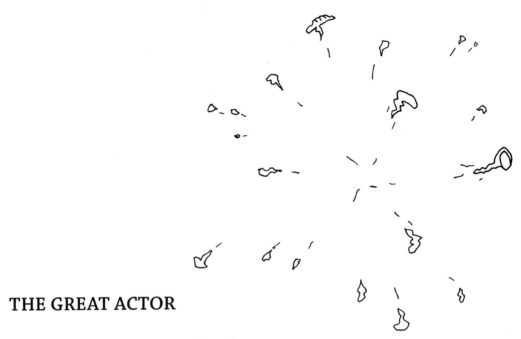

THE GREAT ACTOR

He was the greatest actor of his day
Everyone agreed, everyone said,
Playing such parts as the big brown egg
In the play WHAT THE CHICKEN LAID
And the loaf of bread
In AFTER THE SANDWICHES WERE MADE.

But it was his portrayal of the sugar spoon
In the classic THE SCOLDING TEA,
And his role as the red balloon
In THE TINY PIN'S TERRIBLE DEED
That will really go down in history.

Oh how he is missed
For that last great creation—
Going out with a bang, not a hiss.

Though of course,

Getting a standing ovation.

SUNNY MONEY

I'm building
A ladder
All the way
To the sun.
  I'm not doing it
  Just for fun.
  But for
Pocket money,
    So
    When it's done,
I can charge
  Everyone
  A ton,
  To climb
   All the rungs
And spend
A day
In the sun,
   Sunbathing
On the
    Sun—
   An experience
  Second to none.
(You'll get as
   Brown as a bun!)
   Ho-hum.

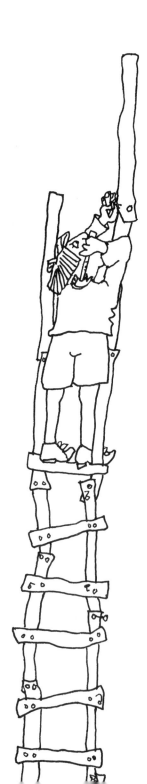

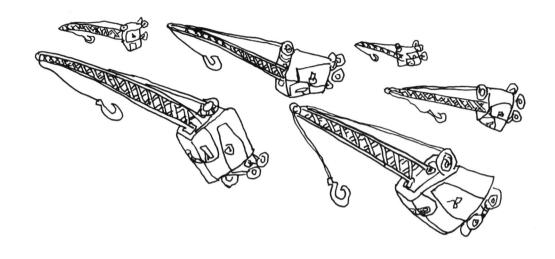

MYSTERIOUS MIGRATION

The migrating cranes are off again!
Rising, a picturesque delight,
From their construction sites
In the deepening evening light.
Off to Spain from the coast of Maine,
Over the trees, the shining sea,
Their graceful hooked beaks,
Their long lithe metal necks—
Oh where will they come to rest?
Where will they build their nests next?

Ah, to see is to believe
One of Mother Nature's mysteries.

THE KING OF POETRY

Oh fiddle dee dee, I do decree,
For I'm the King of Poetry,
Let all my subjects throughout the land
Wax out loud most rapturously
On the buzziness of bees, the trunkiness of trees,
The grittiness of a grain of sand,
Or laze and gaze most frivolously
By the side of a babbling stream.

Oh fiddle dee dee, I do decree,
For I'm the King of Poetry,
Let all my subjects clean their ears
And hear with renewed clarity
The trilling of the lark, the gargling of the shark,
The youthful yodeling of the deer,
And sit on shores of crashing seas
And listen to their symphonies.

Oh fiddle dee dee, I do decree,
For I'm the King of Poetry,
Let all my subjects wear new specs
And see a world like visionaries,
As the cosmos whirls, the stars all turn,
Future lands lay undiscovered yet,
And take their minds to sights unseen
And disappear into their dreams.

Oh fiddle dee dee, I do decree,
For I'm the King of Poetry,
Let all my subjects listen to me
And if they think that flowers pong,
And they're allergic to the nightingale's song,
Then I decree, oh fiddle dee dee,
That they go home before too long,
And turn the TV on.

HOW TO USE A UNICORN

Follow instructions carefully

Say "Sit!"
To unicorn

In middle
Of floor,

Or driveway,
Or lawn.

Pace out five steps
Or more.

Take hoops provided
(Usually four),

Aim, and throw,
That's all.

A game all the family
Will surely adore.

Perfect for parties
Or when thoroughly bored.

Be warned—
Sharp horn.

Careful when bending
Around unicorn.

Rodeo riding and jousting prohibited by law.
Unsuitable for newborns.

BUFFALO OF THE MIND

I'm the Buffalo of the Mind,
Racing across the plains of time.
Running with the herd—

And there you stood, straight and still,
Before my mind, Buffalo Bill,
With your back turned, unconcerned.

Didn't you hear my hooves, that thunderous sound?
Didn't you feel the shudder and trembling of the ground?

Poor ol' Buffalo Bill,
You should have turned round,

Oh you should have turned round.

(Yes, I'm the Buffalo of the Mind,
So don't be a Buffalo Bill.
Watch your behind!)

KID CON

Like to buy some dry water?
One gallon a quarter.
It's very rare
And lighter than air.
Did I hear you say yes?
You're very shrewd, I must confess.
Oh, while you're at it,
How about some Fool's Gold?
Very expensive but worthless I'm told.
But certainly you won't regret a thing—
Oh, and I'll throw in
An invisible diamond ring.
Now, I think that should be enough.
Let's add it up.
Dry water, extra light;
Diamond ring, glittery and bright;
Chunk of very cheap Fool's Gold.
Right. That's all your pocket money you owe.
Okay. Sold!
Now where's the dough?

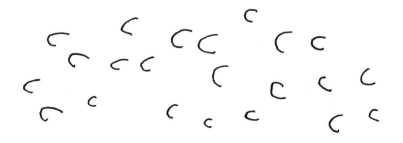

THE LEANING TOWER OF PIZZA

When lovely little Lisa
Went to live in the Leaning Tower of Pizza,
She just sat around reachin'
For another slice of pizza
And watching movies (usually double features).
And very soon our lovely Lisa
Became, what can only be called
A "Pizza Creature,"
Whose features were the size
And consistency of an extra
Large pan-baked pizza.
And oh how her parents
(Even her teachers) beseeched her:
"OH PLEASE LISA, NO MORE PIZZA!"
But their beseechin' didn't reach her.
So she just kept on reachin'
For yet another slice of pizza,
Until that fateful day
As she was reachin'
For a mega-mushroom
'N' overstuffed olive pizza—well . . . eekaa!
On top of Lisa's features
Fell the whole Leaning Tower of Pizza
(Till all you could see were her sneakers).
Oh, and of course, there was much weepin',
And sad and stirring speeches
By both parents and teachers.
But perhaps the preacher
Summed it up best when he said,
"Well, we're all sorry about Lisa.
But I suppose . . . that'll teach her."

COLLABORATION
(To E.P. from me)

Let's write a poem together.

I'll start.

The pygmy is a giant in the ant's world.
The ant is a giant in the microbe's world.
The microbe is a giant in the . . . er . . . er . . .

Okay, now it's your turn.

SLEEP-RUNNER

I don't sleep-walk but sleep-run.
Last night I ran a marathon,

So here in the morning sun
I'm exhausted after my night-long run.
(Even my slippers have holes in 'em.)

But there again, when all's said and done,
As for that marathon—

At least I won.

THE CHARM OF THE NOT SO LITTLE LEPRECHAUN
(For Those About to Doubt)

Oh the charms of little leprechauns,
Twinkly-eyed, cheery—but far, far from large!

Imaginary, mythical, you might say they are
(Grouped with goblins, green men from Mars).

But, ah, just to prove that they really "are"—
Out could leap a leprechaun that's unbelievably

LARGE

(Towering as tall as a double Dutch barn,
Each shoe the size of a cargo barge)

And lift you up with his great big arms
And clang your head upon the stars
And roar in your ear to your utter alarm.
(Before he dunks you into a barrel of lard!)

"NOW DO YOU BELIEVE IN LEPRECHAUNS?"

GET A LIFE!

My shadow—
Oh that copycat!
Always doing the things I do,
Stuck to my feet like glue,
Following me around
Like some shady character, a silly clown.
Oh why can't it have some backbone?
Have some expression of its own?
Like, when I stand, why can't it just sit down?
Or when I stay real still, why doesn't it wave its arms around?
Perhaps then I'd have some respect for it,
And I wouldn't feel embarrassed a bit
Walking around with it.
But stuck here on my heels!
Hey, GET A LIFE! GET REAL!

WASTED WATER

To drink from
The Fountain of Youth,
This I'm told,
You have to travel
Down that road
For many a year or so.

And when,
In front of the fountain
You eventually stop,
You're much too
Tired and old
(Believe it or not)
To lift your little cup
And drink
A single drop.

LEAPING LEMMINGS
and the "Anti-Splat Pack"
(Patent pending)

Oh pity those poor little lemmings,
While running towards the sea,
Eager to get their whiskers wet,
Leap over cliffs and wh

e

e

e

.

.

.

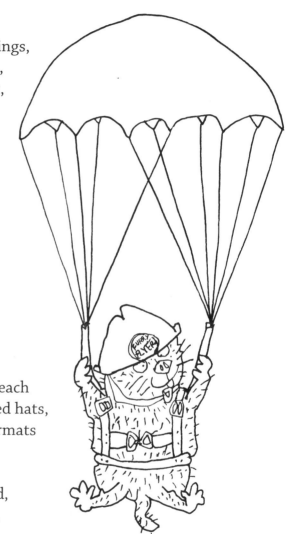

But rather than lazing on the beach
In deckchairs and wide-brimmed hats,
Find themselves like furry doormats
Laid out pancake flat.

So to come to the lemmings' aid,
And to stop them going SPLAT,
How about little parachutes
For their little lemming backs?
(And perhaps even little hardhats
Color-coordinated to match?)

How's that?

A CURE FOR CHILDREN ON TOAST

Let the dragon boast
To being immortal, or living longer than most.
Let the dragon boast
That a long life comes from those it roasts.
In fact, exclusively little children
Roasted on buttered toast.

Oh but let us change the dragon's tune,
So come tomorrow morning or the afternoon,
It will have no breakfast or dinner, too.
For let us coat ourselves in glutinous goo
And smelly stuff from head to shoe,
So even a dragon will go, "Oh my goodness! Poo!"

And refuse to eat (hurrah!)
A single child for many a day,
Till wafer thin it wastes away
And thus will never ever boast
How it is immortal or lives longer than most,
And how it pops poor children down its throat
On slabs of buttered toast.

(And perhaps then
We can stop wearing this awful goo
And there won't be a chorus of "Poo!"
Wherever we happen to go, too.)

NO MAN'S LAND

I journeyed into No Man's Land
And there surprisingly, I met a man
Who said his name was Noman.
"Don't you mean Norman?"
"Norman? No, Noman!
For surely you understand
That's why I call this land
Noman's Land not Norman's Land.
Norman's, not Noman's Land—
Wouldn't be normal," said Noman.

Luckily I met a man, not a woman, in Noman's Land;
Otherwise, things might have been much more difficult to understand.

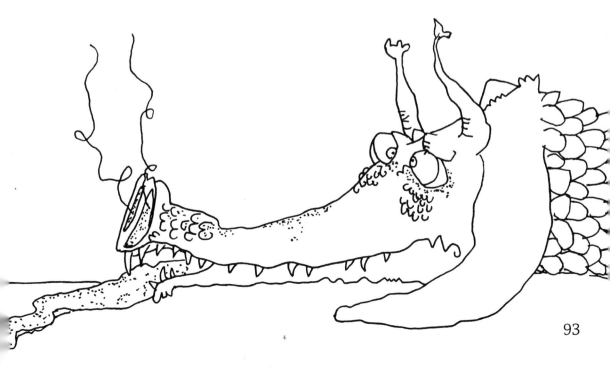

EXTRA ASSISTANCE

When Mister Magic sawed his assistant in half,
    the audience laughed.

When he sawed her in quarters,
    they gasped.

When he sawed her in eighths,
They screamed, "NO, PLEASE WAIT!"

"Wait?" said Mister Magic. "But I don't think I ought t'.
I need more assistants, even though they'll be shorter."

THE BOY WHO CRIED,
"THE FIVE-HUNDRED-HEADED WORMS ARE COMING!"
(The Same Boy Who Cried "Wolf!")

When the boy cried,
"The eyeball-eating ants are coming!"
"The eyeball-eating ants are coming!"
Everyone came running,
Thinking they could be of help,
But found the boy there smiling to himself.

When the boy cried,
"The deadly poisonous piranhas are coming!"
"The deadly poisonous piranhas are coming!"
Everyone came running
Thinking they could be of help,
But found the boy there smiling to himself.

When the boy cried,
"The ferocious fire-breathing raccoons are coming!"
"The ferocious fire-breathing raccoons are coming!"
Everyone came running
Thinking they could be of help
But found the boy there smiling to himself.

When the boy cried,
"The five-hundred-headed worms are coming!"
"The five-hundred-headed worms are coming!"
Yeah, right . . . five-hundred-headed worms?
Still, everyone came running when they heard—
Amazingly, some people never learn!

SLOW COACH CHARLIE

Slow Coach Charlie, the great athlete,
Unbelievably slow upon his feet,
Has entered the Slow Olympic Games
Looking for recognition, glory, and fame
In the 100 meters Super Slow Sprint.
(Very exciting for snails, I think.)

Of course, they've already said, "Ready, Steady, Go!"
And off they went (slowly) quite some time ago.
Charlie's in the lead (that means he's last).
He's beating Slothman Sam, who's a little too fast.

But the winning post is a long way off,
So you'd better not hold your breath.
Though if you want to pick a winner,
Slow Coach is a pretty good bet.

Oh the excitement is really building,
The slow sprinters are sweaty 'n' hot.
Maybe there'll be a winner (next week),
But, then again . . . maybe not.

A SHORT SAD SONG

A grasshopper
Asked whether,
By rubbing its legs together,
It could join our choir.

But sadly
It didn't stay long,
For after only one song,
It caught fire.

BUGGED BUGS

In today's technological times,
They're teaching bugs to be spies—

Highly trained beetles and butterflies,

Who can go on special missions
Behind enemy lines,

Are prepared to be squashed, to die,

Just to bring back classified secret info—
Stuff us humans would love to know,

Like, how many flowers there are in Asia
Or whether bees have nuclear lasers.

INSECT INNOCENCE

Said the spider to the little fly,
"Come into my parlor
Where we can sit and sumptuously dine."

"Dine on me, surely you mean," replied the little fly.

"Who on earth do you think I am?"
Said the spider. "I've soft-boiled yams,
Freshly baked clams and home-made jam
And tea-leaf treacle wine. Oh, on these we'll surely dine."

"Oh, how divine," said the little fly.
"Then, naturally, that's fine."

And innocently went inside.

THE TALLNESS OF A WALL

If I were tall, far taller than this wall,
I'd be able to see the Phantom Fjords, the Shoe Shop Shores,
And the In-Between Ends for sure.
I'd be able to see the butterblops who dress in kitchen mops
In cities glittering like sugary buns—
A skyline of oversized wellingtons
And matching sets of minarets
With cherries on the top.

And if I were tall, far taller than this wall,
I'd be able to see those animals roam: the Tuffulut, the Fluffalot,
And the Shortened Truncated Sload.
I'd be able to see their necks in knots, all elongated and squat,
Billowing beasts with feathered feet
Who graze on whatnot sweets
And dance the Doodle, the Stodgy Strudel,
And waggle their spotted bots.

And if I were tall, far taller than this wall,
I'd be able to see the Furniture Forests, the Pillow Plains,
And the Deserts of Continual Rain.
I'd be able to see the icebergs covered with tropical birds,
Clothes-horses cantering to the summer sales,
And seas of earthbound weeping whales,
Where thousands of caroling children
Can be seen but never heard.

Ah, but when I really am tall, far taller than this wall,
Will the Fluffalot still roam and roar and the hedgesplodge softly call?
Will the Doodle be forgotten for sure and the Tuffulut be no more?
Oh as I grow up, will all go down
To the other side of Nowhere Now
And disappear with a sort of soggy sandwichy sound?

For I bet when I eventually look over this wall,
There'll be nothing there at all!

THE WHOLE TRUTH AND NOTHING BUT THE TRUTH

It's said
That in the deepest jungles
There are butterflies
The size of bedspreads,
Like vampire bats
But twice as fat,
That swoop down
And in your hair
Lay their eggs.
And when they hatch,
The caterpillars
Bite off your head.

But how can you
Possibly believe that?
Yes, okay, twice as fat
As vampire bats,
But I know for a fact
That these flying
Butterfly bedspreads
Swoop down
In the night instead
And swallow you up whole
While you're asleep in bed.

Sometimes the truth is hard to believe,
Even when it comes from me!

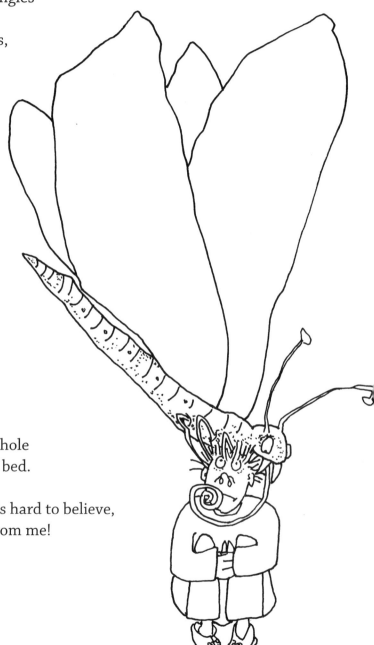

COMCUTERS

In the future
We'll be like computers

(But cuter)

And they'll be able
To switch us on.

And before long,

We'll be programmed
With lots of clever stuff,

Until someone says,
"I think this one's had enough."

And away we'll go
With high IQs.

And what's really cool—
We'll never ever have to

Go to school!

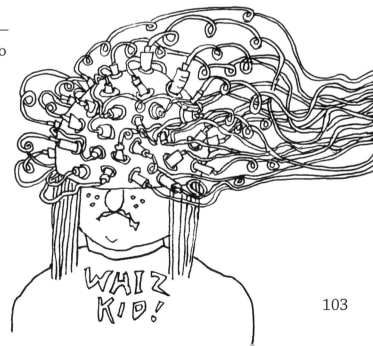

OH GOSH, THE SPLOSH!

SQUELCH, SQUELCH, SQUELCH, the Splosh
Comes sloshing out of the sea—oh, gosh!
A scaly, whaley, fat 'n' flabby thing
Whose body is bulbous 'n' blubbery,
Whose mouth is wrinkled 'n' rubbery,
A slimy submariney sort of thing
With floppy floundery fins.

And it comes across the beach,
And on and on down the street,
With its skin seaweedy 'n' soggy,
With its breath diabolically boggy,
With its boots full of slopping water,
As it lurches 'n' searches for moms 'n' dads
And their tender young sons 'n' daughters.

And all that is heard is

SQUELCH . . . SQUELCH . . . SQUELCH . . .

Till "OH GOSH, IT'S THE SPLOSH! HELP!"

Then . . . nothing else

But . . . BELCH!

And . . . SQUELCH . . .   SQUELCH . . .   SQUELCH . . .

SIDE-STEPPING STORY

Giving directions to a crab
Is as frustrating as it is sad—

"Right, just go straight till you cross . . ."
Well, you just know it's going to get lost.

SQUELCH . . .   SQUELCH . . .   SQUELCH . . .

FRESHLY BREWED BLOOM

The miniature Darjeeling Lotus
Grows practically unnoticed
Upon the surface of nice, hot tea.
A brownish bloom, difficult to see,
But before you've noticed it in your cup,
You've already gone and drunk it up.

JUGGLING CUDDLING CREATURE

I tell no lies—
Giant octopi
Have a J and C (even G and D)
Hearing disability.
So when teaching one to juggle,
Don't blame me
If it gets in a bit of a muddle.

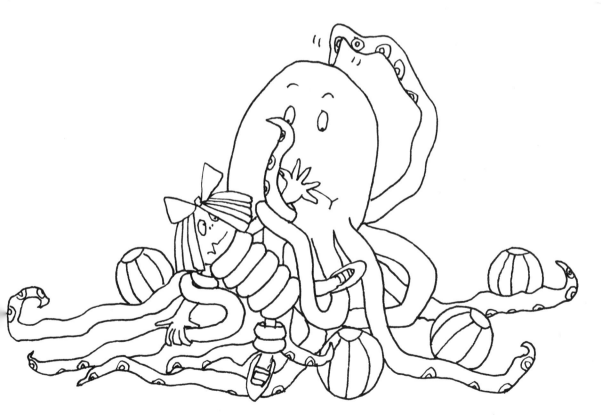

FAMILY ENTERTAINMENT

I have a peculiar father
Who loves to do the splits
And the double backward flip,
Who pogos in the parlor
And cavorts and cartwheels across the lawn
Every morning at the crack of dawn.

Although sometimes I think I'd rather
Have a regular boring father
Who would much prefer to sit,
Who's still a bit of a twit,
But doesn't do the splits
Or double backward flips
And doesn't pogo in the parlor,
Or cartwheel across the lawn
   at the crack of dawn—
One who doesn't embarrass me at all.

And of course, my mother's not much better,
Swinging from the living room trapeze,
Balancing on the banister, juggling cheese . . .
   That is, if only I'd let her.

But I suppose when I'm home alone
With nothing to do, and it's raining,
At least they're entertaining.

THE MAKER OF LAUGHTER

Night after night
The Maker of Laughter
Cries himself to sleep,
Sobbing softly beneath the sheets,
"Everyone's laughing at me. Everyone I meet."

"Yes, I made laughter,
But that ha-ha-ha stuff came after.
I made it all in seriousness
Like any true artist.
But everyone's being contortionists,
Going into fits, acting like complete fools with it—
Rolling around on the floor,
Opening wide their ridiculous jaws—
That wasn't my intention at all!"

"A ha-ha-ha, a he-he-he, a belly-aching roar—
Those should be appreciated
For their sonorous sounds no more.
While a chuckle or a little giggle,
They're the artistic expression of a tickle.
Ah, but nobody understands me.
They think laughing's for joking, you see.
It's always the same with everyone I meet:
'Hey, you made laughter? That's really neat!'
Neat! Neat? It's enough to make a man weep."

And with that, the Maker of Laughter
Draws up the sheets
And, counting laughing sheep,
Cries himself to sleep.

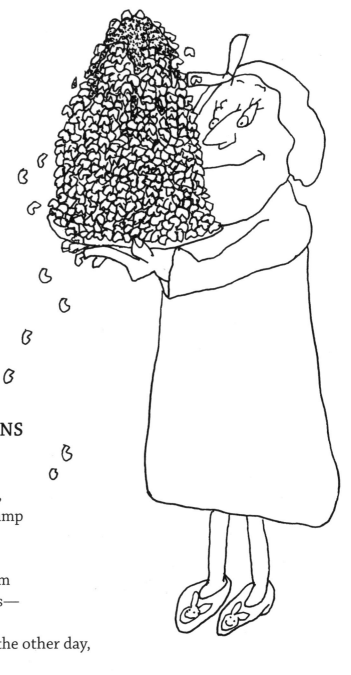

MY HAS-BEEN BEANS

I was given some
Mexican jumping beans,
And I trained them to jump
Higher than any beans
You've ever seen.
I was going to enter them
Into the Olympic Games—
That was my dream.
But when I came home the other day,
I really couldn't believe,
For supper, my mother had made for me,
Mexicana Bean Supreme.
Well, I think that was really mean!

HAPPY HOUR

Hey, it's Happy Hour!
When everyone must be happy,
When everyone has to laugh and smile,
Dance and do cartwheels and flips.
And frolic, be funny, have giggling fits,
And go "Whoopee!" and "Yippee!"
And be incredibly happeeeee!
For Happy Hour is here,
So let's smile from ear to ear.

Until . . . in a little while,
We can forget all about these silly smiles,
'Cause Horrid Hour will be here.
And then we can be nice 'n' nasty 'n' weird.
Oh, and also very shortly,
We can be really, really naughty
Misbehaving little rascals
Who never do anything that anyone asks us
And play horrid tricks on all our friends
In the hope that Horrid Hour will never end.

POTTED PERSONALITY

The Flowerpot People
Are a dull and mysterious lot.
But occasionally, mysteriously,
Sometimes they're not.
For as strange as it may sound,
It's been clearly found
That by turning their world upside down,
Very soon—in, say, a day or two—
Their personalities bloom,
And they brighten up too.

HUNTING THE WILD, WILD WIND

I'm off to hunt the wild wind—
To catch it, trap it,
And rope it in.

So I've brought along some wind-trapping things:
An umbrella to be turned all inside out.
Newspapers to be blown about.
A hat to be knocked completely off.
And a couple of lids of bins.

And when I eventually hunt that wild wind down,
I'll rope it, truss it round and round,
Then tame it from a biting blustery breed
To a soft and gentle summer breeze.

And I'll keep it as a pet,
And now and again I'll let
It whistle a little tune,
Chase a colored balloon,
Or quietly play there in the air.

And if it's really good . . . it can ruffle my hair.

THE GREATEST

He was by far the greatest boxer
That the world had ever seen.
Knocking out the big, the brutal,
And even the extremely mean.

Not by speed or subtle skills,
But when the bell went "DING!"
He could simply knock them out
From the other side of the ring.

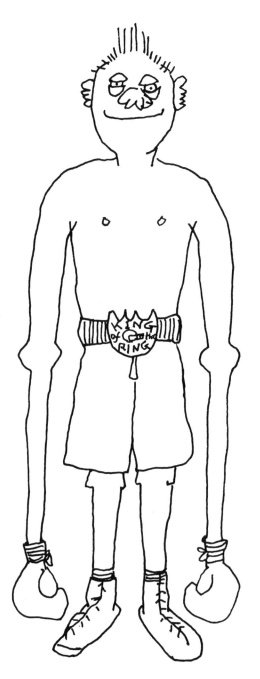

ROBINSON OF UNREALITY

A poor castaway was he,
Lost in the vast nothingness of sea,
East by southwest but further north—
Somewhere out there between the poles
Where the winds blow hot and cold,
Stranded miles off course.

A poor castaway in time,
Each second ticking down an eternal line.
Forgotten in the swirling mist,
Washed up on an empty beach
Where civilization had yet to reach,
And where, oh how he wished,

He didn't have to talk to the fish!
That his parrot wasn't the one he kissed.
That there was someone else around.
That he could cut his knee-length hair,
And have new clothes to wear,
And with good fortune he'd be found.

Oh, a castaway on a distant shore,
Until . . . until Mrs. Wopple knocked on his door
To borrow a bowl of sugar and an egg
And invite him round for a bite to eat,
Perhaps meet the neighbors down the street.
"Your parrot's invited too," she said.

Oh, a poor castaway indeed was he,
But as you can see, the Robinson of Unreality.

BEWARE THE POLAR BEAR

(Arctic or Armchair)

Over this white and wintery world
There sits the polar bear,
As proud a portrait of a beast
To grace this frozen lair,
Who smiles a beam, a beacon bright,
All visitors beware—
A smile to announce, "I'll eat you alive,
Suddenly, unseasoned, and rare."

But let us take our polar bear
And place it in an old armchair,
Slippers, and a dressing gown.
Perhaps a pipe, let's part its hair.
By a fireplace, suburban snug,
Sipping tea from china ware,
While on its knees a TV dinner,
Something unseasoned and rather rare.

Gone that regal sovereign pose,
Gone the king of icy lairs,
Gone the beast whose burdens now
Are which pajamas should it wear.
But ah, that smile, that smile survives.
That smile that's always there,
Announcing "Beware the polar bear,
Arctic or armchair."
That smile that curves and cuts the air.
"All visitors (all children) beware—
I'll eat you alive, suddenly, unseasoned, and rare."

So please, take care!

YOU'RE FAR TOO YOUNG
AND OTHER FEEBLE EXCUSES

(Or How to Lie to a Firefly)

When the firefly
Applied for a job

As a fireman,

Instead of 'em saying,
"Son, that's just plain dumb,"

They told it,
"You're far too young

And, sorry, but
(Here's another feeble excuse)

The job's already gone to a moose
Who plays the flute and juggles fruit."

REMEMBRANCE OF THINGS FAST

I remember when the world was fast—
Wow, so much faster than it is now.
Night and day would be the wink of an eye.
You just can't imagine the speed of time—
Seasons would simply fly right by.
There would be sixteen a year, and that's no lie.
An hour would seem like a single second,
A month just a week, I reckon.
The world would revolve at an incredible speed.
Ah yes, those were the days for me.

Whatever happened to time's runaway race?
It's all slowed down to a real snail's pace.
Everything's moving as if it's stuck in glue,
Crawling around, nearly at a standstill, too.
Time's surely not exercising. It's obviously unfit.
It used to make me giddy and really sick,
But now it's gone all sleepy and sluggish.
I really don't know what's wrong with it.

Maybe the world's just gone and got old—
That's why it's so very slow and, oh,
It's just got tired of going round and round.
Perhaps time needs some time to go and lie down.
It's funny, I'm still as sprightly and as young as ever.
I'll never slow down. Never! Never!
But it's a pity about the world, though. I feel sorry for it.
Of course, I suppose I could always lend it my walking stick
While I go and sit down for a bit.

BATTY

Bats—the vampire sort—
Of course, have a similar name to "bats" (the ones for sport).
So be careful when playing, say, baseball, which requires a bat.
For instead of it going "WHACK!"
The bat might not do that.
It might go "WHIZZZ" (like a bat out of hell),
And, well, I know it's sometimes hard to tell,
But here's the simple fact—
You picked the wrong kind of bat!

MIGHTY MOUTHY MOUSE

Nicknamed "The Little Munching Machine,"
The Long-Nosed Mouthy Mouse
Is a furry friend who should surely
Never ever visit your house,
For rather than scratching under floorboards,
Or chewing holes in your living room walls,
Instead of leaving carpets nicely nibbled and gnawed,
In days it will leave you . . . with no house at all!

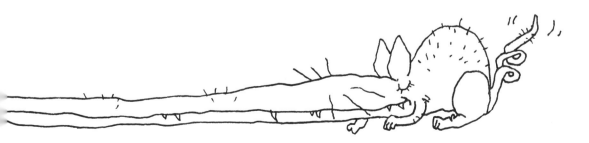

THE MAGIC OF MOTHER

There I was lying on my bed,
Thinking of doing nothing much instead,
When my mom said, "Oh, since you're here,
I have the most marvelous, fantastic idea.
If you'd like all your wishes granted, my dear,
Then take this magic lamp and rub it,
And a genie will appear.
Oh, and while you're at it,
Take this magic pot and scrub it,
And a genie will appear.
Oh, and while you're at it,
Take this magic silver and polish it,
And a genie will appear.
Oh, and while you're at it,
Take this magic rug and wallop it,
And a genie will appear.

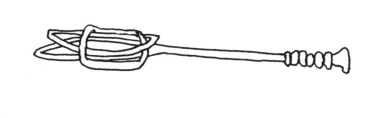

Oh, and while you're at it,
Take this magic mop and clean the floor,
And a genie will appear.
Oh, and while you're at it,
Take this magic broom and sweep the hall,
And a genie will appear.
Oh, and while you're at it, my dear . . ."
Oh dear! Oh dear! Oh dear!
I know one thing is very clear.
If my mom has anything to do with it, I fear,
It's going to be years and years and years
Before that genie ever appears!
(And when it does, I'm going to box its genie ears.)

P.S.
Do you think Aladdin had a problem like this
Every time he wanted to make a wish?

THE SLUDGIE

Slowly the sludgie
(Something between a slug and a budgie)
Comes crawling across the sky
On the underside of clouds,
Emitting loud sucking sounds
And winking its beady eyes.

It's a thing extremely slimy
That fumbles along blindly,
Rather like an enormous stain
That gulps and burps and swallows.
It's almost completely hollow—
Just a stomach without a brain.

And when buffeted in stormy weather,
This bag of slime and feathers,
From the clouds it becomes unstuck,
To land in the ocean like an oil slick
(If you swim in it, it'll make you sick),
Or on land like a pool of muck.
And if you step in it . . . YUCK!

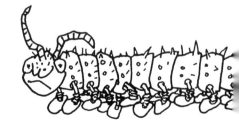

PITY ME, THE CENTIPEDE

Oh pity me, the centipede,
Of troubles I must speak.

Oh pity me, the centipede,
The one with a hundred feet.

Oh pity me, the centipede,
Who must polish one hundred shoes.

Oh pity me, the centipede;
Who washes a hundred socks, too.

Oh pity me, the centipede,
Whose one hundred feet I foolishly felt.
(And whose same hundred socks I certainly smelt!)

Oh pity me, the centipede,
When today I turned and walked over myself.

THE QUEEN BEE AND THE KINGFISHER

The queen bee and the kingfisher,
A most royal but irregular pair,
But somehow there was perfection
In the way they ruled the air.

They lived down by the river
In a lovely little hive.
She'd sit home making honey,
And into the water he'd dive.

And he'd bring her little fishes
With a flash of his blue-backed wings.
She'd say, "How very sweet, my dear.
For you, here's a little sting."

And she'd busily buzz about the house
Humming her little honey song.
And he'd sit by the shining water
As the shadows of life grew long.

Oh the queen bee and the kingfisher,
A most royal but irregular pair,
But somehow there was perfection
In the way they ruled the air.

PRUNE TUNE

Wrinkled, wrinkled, little prune,
Oh so wrinkled on my spoon.

We get wrinkles under eyes
When we're old—say ninety-nine.

Wrinkled, wrinkled, little prune,
Better get some prune cream soon!

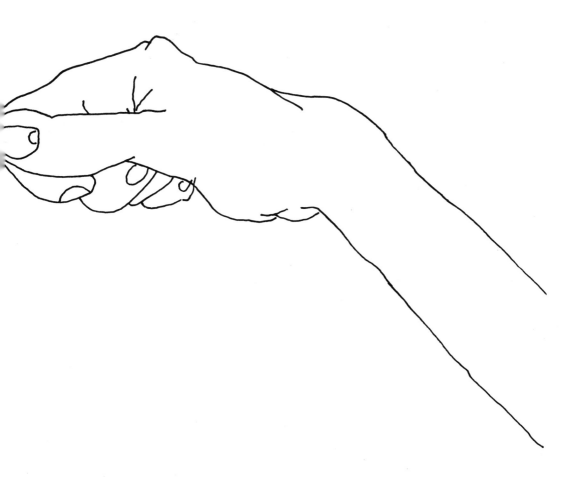

THE BUILDERBEAST

Of the builderbeast I now do speak—
A creature half bird, half beast,
Who builds its architectural oddities
'Cross the mysterious lands of the East.
Towers, minarets, vast cities of silly shapes,
That it weaves with its long curved beak.

Atop a tower it lays its hard-boiled eggs,
Then waits patiently for them to hatch,
Though after several years, it dries its tears
And then simply lays another batch.
Yet still it survives and multiplies,
And that's the mysterious fact.

It flies by walking extremely fast
Across the Earthly Elaborate Plains,
And calls from one of its home-made frames,
Impersonating the London-to-Brighton train.
But as it's never stepped foot in the West,
This is indeed remarkably strange.

So if you ever manage to go due east
And marvel at the palaces and pagodas there,
Marvel not so much at a great emperor's power
Or exotic cultures in raw silken wear—
Marvel rather at the brilliant builderbeast
Up there roaring in its aerial lair.

133

A VERY HIP OPOTAMUS

I own a hip opotamus—
An opotomus, very hip.

It keeps up with the latest styles
Like sequined shirts,
And spotted ties,
'N' floppy hats below the eyes.

Oh my opotomus is very hip,
But not so fashionable, I admit
(Not just a little bit),
When it comes to where it sits.

PINOCCHIOOOOOOOH!

When he said
He could play the cymbals,
Pinocchio lied.
I don't know why.
But he shouldn't have done,
'Cause it can't have been much fun.

(Think about that one.)

MING THING

Nothing is finer
Than a firebird from China
That sits and sweetly sings
Of things mysterious and Ming.

Till yesterday,
I had one of these wonderful birds,
But I don't know whether you've heard.
This morning when I awoke,
Sadly, I'm afraid to say,
My firebird was just a cloud of smoke.

THE REAL STORY
(When Romance Goes Radically Wrong)

He never wanted to be a handsome prince.
He much preferred the life of a big, fat, lazy frog.
All the royal ceremonies and duties, the snobby regal lot
He would trade in a second for that pond, that little log,
Where he'd sit and eternally croak. Oh that life he missed!
Oh why, oh why had he ever been kissed?

But being a princess wasn't what it was all made out to be—
All the curtsying and coyness and unbelievably boring balls.
She'd much prefer to sit by that pond with froggy dear.
Oh that gorgeous green skin, those big bulging eyes she adored.
Ah, that handsome face, that pompous profile. It made her wince.
She was in love with a frog, not a stupid prince!

IT'S ALWAYS WORSE
FOR CAPTAIN CURSE

"Aaah, it's either an attack of termites
In this wretched wooden leg,
Or a case of runaway rust
On m' ol' hooked hand instead."

"I'm rotten from top to bottom—
No wonder they call me Captain Curse,
Living with this question-mark of a hand,
Like some hobblin' hop-along man—
Aaah, things just couldn't get worse."

That is until Pudgy Polly, the captain's pet albatross
(Uh-oh, the Bird of Doom!), took flight
(His parrot had died from rust and termites)
And carried him screaming,
"Oh shiver me timbers, I spoke too soon!"—
To the utter astonishment of his crew—
Up and away without a trace
Into the seven starry seas of space.

WHEN BIRDBRAIN BECAME TAME

(Or What's in a Name?)

(Or . . . Oh My Golly, Someone Thinks He's Pudgy Polly!)

Albert Tross thought himself a bird,
One with the biggest wingspan in the world,
When to everyone's alarm,
He would flap both his arms
And generally act absurd.

Until one day he changed his name
To Arma Dillow and suddenly became
Withdrawn, in a shell—
Shyly spoken as well,
As if all his wild ways were tamed.
(Though to his friends he was just as strange.)

Still, most preferred the old Albert Tross
And often bemoaned his loss.

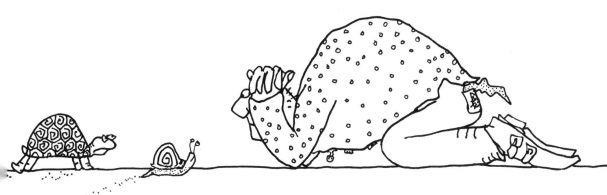

JACK AND JILL

It's not so nice
Being Jill, ol' Jack Frost's wife,
Who's forever catching frostbite
When Jack kisses her goodnight.
Her lips are frozen white,
Her face, a sheet of ice—
Oh what a sight.
Oh what a life!
Being poor Jill Frost,
Ol' Jack Frost's wife.

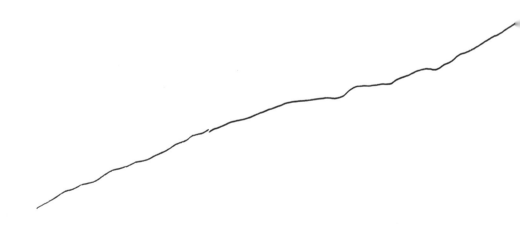

PROMISE TO A PEAK

Oh Mighty Mountain,
Hear me speak,
For I have vowed to conquer you.
And this I've promised, this I'll do—
To scale your lonely lofty ledges,
Your towering snowy peak,
Oh Mighty Mountain,
Hear me speak.

Oh Mighty Mountain,
Hear these words,
For I have vowed to conquer you.
To stand atop your distant world,
This I've promised, this you've heard.
Sometime soon
Or sometime later,
But probably when
You've an elevator.

WHEN LEFT AND RIGHT DISAGREED
ON THE WAY TO THE CHINA SEA

A pair of shoes set out one day,
One left and, of course, one right.
Laces loose and happily heeled—
Oh indeed, what a pleasant sight.

"We're off to see the China Sea
And dance upon the beach."
As they skipped on nimbly down the road,
For soon the sea they'd reach.

But lo, they came to a fork in that road,
And there they disagreed,
One saying left, the other right
'Bout the way to the China Sea.

So thus they parted company,
Left choosing left, quite naturally,
While right stepped right and headed off,
Somewhat self-righteously.

And there, eventually, was the sea.
The right shoe nodded knowingly,
While on and on the left shoe strode
Through strange and barren scenery.

Through mountains, deserts, jungles deep,
The left shoe sought to roam,
With never a sign of the China sea,
To be left there all alone.

But there on the beach the right shoe danced
As stars bloomed bright that night,
Smiling contentedly to itself
With the knowledge it would always,

ALWAYS be right.

(And by the way, that's all there's left to say!)

SHOCK ON THE SHORE

The fingers of the palm-tree
Wiggle in the wind.
On the shore it waves
To draw all sailors in.

But there upon the beach,
Shrouded in the mist,
Far from a helping hand,
They discover a fearful fist.

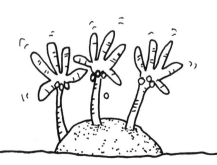

CHINA SEA

THE MUFFIN PUFFIN

Never leave a freshly baked tray of muffins
(That you were planning to have for tea)
At the edge of the beautiful briny sea
To cool in the soft summer breeze

For there, proud as puff pastry, will appear
The magnificent muffin puffin.
And puffin' out its plumage in mock rage
(It's really just bluffin'),
It will swoop down on that tray.

And with a beak like an open oven door
And those tremendous dough-kneading claws,
It will snatch your bake day right away,
And there on the shore your muffins will be no more.

Oh beware of the muffin puffin
(Whose feathery face it's always stuffin'),
'Cause one minute you'll have muffins
And the next you'll have nuffin'.

ELECTRICKY DICKY,
THE 100-WATT BOY

Electricky Dicky's a "shocker"
In every sense of the word.
One touch with his little finger,
And v-v-v-v-volts he will transfer
To spike your hair like toothbush bristles
And make your eyelashes frizzle.

Boy or bulb or living battery?
All innocent, elecri-cute.
But shake his hand, and there you'll be,
Abuzz from brow to boots.
Down the spine all shocks 'n' shivers,
Teeth a-chatter, tongue aquiver.

Still, if you want to save a dime
And cut down on lighting costs,
Inviting Electricky 'round for dinner
Would never be a loss.
For he makes a lovely lamp,
Standing, all static and sparks,
A bright and brilliant 100-watt boy
Glowing in the dark.

WORRYING WHISKERS

How come my cat's got
Whiskers and I have not?

Are they special antennae
Connected to the inner mind,
Transmitting lots of lickin' lingo
And catty comments behind
My back to other catty cousins
And catty nieces and nephews who
Laugh and call me names
Like "two-legged lanky bird-brain"
And plan to take over the world—
And worse yet, give me a collar
And make me their pet?

Just to think of all those little catty communications
Whizzing through the air
Makes me worried, makes me really scared.

Oh if only I had whiskers too!
I could then know what my cat knew too.
And see right through his little plans
And . . . make plans of my very own
Before he and his cousins
Take over my home.

THE MARVELS OF THE MEDICINE MAN

Gather round, ladies and gents—
For all of you whose ears are unscrewed
Or who fret if your tonsils are bent,
I've got medicine here that's heaven-sent.

Firstly folks, you just have to try this—
"The Fantastic Fixer," the amazing elixir
That's undoubtedly the perfect cure
For those who have fallen down sewers
And smell of old socks and manure.
Ah and this, just one sniff from this bottle
And every cell in your body will work at full throttle.
Or rub this incredible ointment
All over your heels and elbows.
Not only will you grow an inch or so,
But it will frighten away the crows.

Oh, and this rare exotic extract
From the root of the "Wonder Weed"
Is excellent for wobbly knees
And backward blinking disease.
(Though one drop of it in the bath,
And you'll be immediately immune to sharks.)
A-ha, and the contents of this little green jar
Will put mega-muscles in skinny thin arms
And a head of hair on each of your palms.
Oh, and here's a special offer, folks
(Only three for the price of four)—
A cream for stopping hiccups
And from walking into doors.
And wait, don't go yet—
I've plenty more, you bet!
I've boxes and boxes of pills
For all you who have never been ill.
And lastly but not least, oh, here's some
Of my Marvelous Miracle Medicine.
A product second to none,
Rather like liquid chewing gum.
Just rub some on your tum
Or better still, take a teaspoon every night,
And trust me, it will cure you
Even if you're perfectly all right!

PUSH-A-PET

You didn't know this, I bet.

Now you can really get
Vending machines for pets.

At the push of a little button,
You can get a turtle or a cat.

Or if you so desire,
A cuddly vampire bat,

Or a poodle, or a penguin,
Or a squawking cockatoo.

The only problem is
It's so difficult to choose.

NURSERY RHYME FOR A
TWENTY-THREE-TOED TROLL

This little piggy went to market.
This little piggy stayed in bed.
This little piggy made fresh mud pies.
This little piggy looked for truffles instead.
This little piggy lived in Porky Palace.
This little piggy had a smelly straw house.
This little piggy nibbled lettuce leaves.
This little piggy pigged-out.
This little piggy rolled around in the muck.
This little piggy stayed spotlessly clean.
This little piggy was as big as a barrel.
This little piggy was fashionably lean.
This little piggy wore a huge hog hat.
This little piggy wore a curly-whirly wig.
This little piggy did the piggy polka.
This little piggy did an Irish jig.
This little piggy had black and brown spots.
This little piggy was plum-blossom pink.
This little piggy was pampered and perfumed.
This little piggy—oh, what a stink!
And this little piggy simply squeaked and squealed.
And this little piggy just grunted and groaned.
And this little piggy, oh, all on its own,
Cried "wee, wee, wee, wee," all the way home.

SNIFFS AT SEA

On the sailor's nose
Was an apple-pie tattoo,

So he could smell home-cooking
When the sea winds blew.

HOME COOKING
UMM...

IMPRINT OF INDECISION

Within the rock, a fossil.
A footprint—colossal—
Left by the long lost ten-toed tribe
Who lived but sadly died
Never knowing which way to go,
Dithering to and fro, and so
Ending up enclosed in stone.

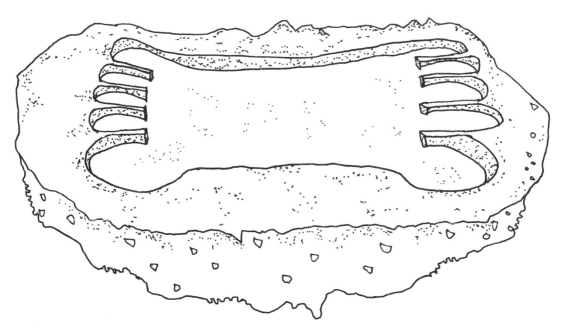

THE ART OF YODEL-ODEL-ODELING

To yodel correctly
You must have
An extremely long neck
And a mouth shaped
Like the entrance to a tunnel.
And you must take in a big breath
And let it out
Like the smoke from a ship's funnel.

And not only must you have a long neck,
But you must have a barrel chest
And a long tongue like a gecko.
And it helps if you're Swiss
And live in the Alps,
Where the mountains
Bounce about with echoes.

But . . . but as none of the above applies to me,
Would you like to hear me gargle with tea?

ANIMAL ORBITS

On the Planet of Cats,

Cats are purring and parading,
Cats are meowing and mauling.
Cats are scratching and screeching,
Cats are lolling and licking,
Cats are padding and pawing.

Cats are furry and fluffy and fabulously feline.
Cats are taily and whiskery and winkingly green-eyed.
Oh and much more of this and that,
Up there on the Planet of Cats.

While on the Planet of Dogs,

Dogs are . . . completely silent!

Not a bark, a howl, a bow-wow, a single sniff.
Nothing doggy at all like this,
'Cause the dogs are too busy looking at their maps.
Studying the position of the Planet of Cats.
Spying through telescopes, checking the zodiac,
Gazing into the heavens, into the starry skies.

For they know that for the cats
There's going to be a big surprise,

When tomorrow night—

The planets collide.

SCARIEST SCARECROW

The scariest scarecrow ever known
Could make you shake down in your bones.
Those evil eyes, that dark satanic smile,
Could frighten everything for miles and miles.
Could frighten the cows and pigs in the corn,
Could frighten the sun from the sky at dawn,
Could frighten you so you could never sleep,
Could frighten you so you could hardly speak.
Could frighten old men till they almost died,
Could frighten the bravest till, like babies, they cried.
Could frighten the leaves right off the trees,
Could frighten the butterflies and bumblebees,
Could frighten the life out of a solid stone.
Could frighten absolutely everything, I suppose.
Well, maybe, but maybe that's not quite so . . .
Everything, that is, except the crows!

ELEPHANTASTIC

Consider the Eleph Ant
As an elephant that has shrunk.
For it can stand there on one leg
And balance a ball upon its trunk,
It can entertain all the circus folk
Doing tricks with a skipping rope,
And even leap through miniature hoops
Of dancing flames and smoke.

So, if you really want to go
To this "Tiny Jumbo Show,"
I wouldn't say no, but oh, I hope
You remember to take your telescope.

COME ON AIR, I'M PREPARED

Today, the weatherman said
The rain would be really hard,
That I should watch out for shooting stars
(Very dangerous, they are!),
That I'll be knocked out by the sun's heat,
That a strong wind will batter and beat
      me on the street.
That a comet might club me,
That the snow might slug me,
That a blizzard might bug me,
That a monsoon might mug me.
So come on, I'm ready, weather.
(Whether you are, or whether you're not.)
Come on air, foul or fair—
I'm prepared . . .
Beat me up if you dare!

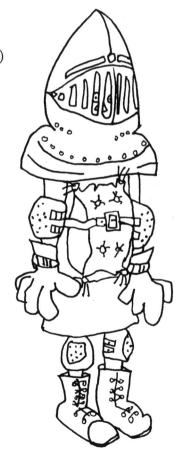

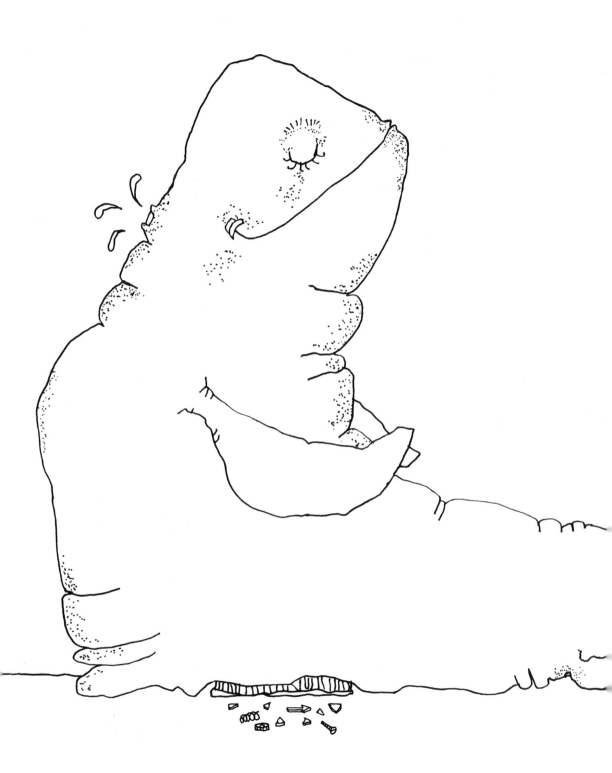

SKINNY DIPPING

When Waddleton Whale
Got on the scales,
He closed his eyes.
Or if he'd put on
A pound or two, he simply lied
About dipping into
The cookie jar of the sea
Or having an extra scoop
Of plankton ice-cream
And pretended he was on a diet
Of salt water and seaweed.
But really he paid diets little heed
For he surely was the most gigantibus
Gulpumphious munchmungerous breed
In all of the seventy seven seas.

But of course, no one actually knew
What Waddleton weighed from spout to tail,
For whenever he approached the scales
And sat on 'em,
He always flattened 'em.

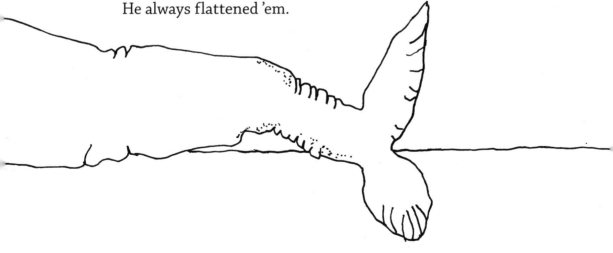

THE LEAF THAT LAUGHED

The little leaf laughed and left its branch,
And as it floated and fluttered away I heard it say,
"Now I'm free! Free to flutter the world forever and a day,
To float away to distant lands, across great wide wondrous seas,
Where I'll see all the things other leaves won't ever see,
And all those unlucky look-alike leaves
Will be so amazed and so jealous of me."

And he laughed and fluttered away,
Saying, "And when I've floated away,
And seen the world forever and a day . . .
When I've seen everything and all,
Then maybe I'll flutter back, maybe in the Fall.
And then at last I'll come back to visit that boring branch—
Well, maybe." And again he laughed.

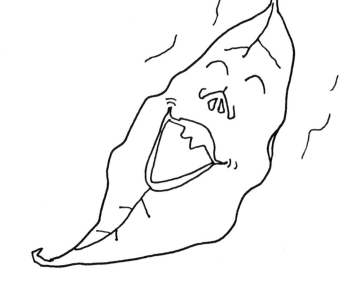

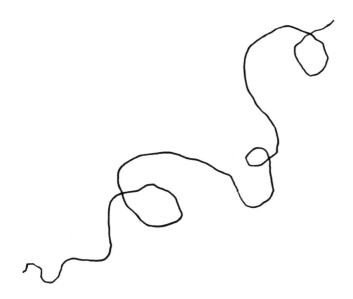

Um . . .
Oh little leaf, oh little leaf—
I'm afraid life's not like that.
There's no floating or fluttering back.
Once you leaf (I mean leave),
You leaf (I mean leave)
So little leaf, oh little leaf,
So naive, so cute,
If ever we meet, little leaf,
I'm going to have to tell you the truth!

Oh little leaf, little leaf,
Your tree days are in the past.
You might leave and laugh—but wait, not so fast,
For I'm afraid it'll be that boring branch
That will have the very last laugh.

SOUL-SEARCHING
OVER SQUAWKING SANDWICHES

Under the moon,
We foxes meet—
The dilemma of dinner:
Oh what to eat?

A plate of treats
From the farmer's house?
A squawking sandwich?
A feathered take-out?

But the guilt we feel
Within our souls,
Can this be "right"
If the truth be told?

Is all this thieving
Of fluffy fast-food,
Plump beak-burgers,
That clucking brood,

Too crafty, too cruel?
A life of deceit?
Oh what if these shoes
Were on other feet?

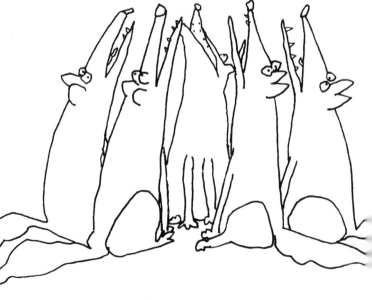

Would not indeed
Our bushy tails tremble
As nipped by frost
In mid-December?

Would we not fear
For life's little lot?
Would we ever again
Dance the famed fox-trot?

Oh how our bellies rumble,
Oh how our mouths water,
As the long night grows shorter
Over all this oughtn't or ought t'.

To do or not to do,
On this we must surely muse,
As under the silvery moon
We sadly howl the blues.

While far away,
Warm and snug
In straw-soft beds,
Tightly tucked,

Those snoozing sandwiches
Sweet sheep they count.
And roosting there,
Those fat take-outs

Sleep on and on
In the farmer's house,
Not knowing or caring
What all the fuss is about.

OL' JELLYFISH FACE

Ol' jellyfish face
Was a favorite with the kids
For all the contortions
And impressions he did.

Living, laughing jelly;
A wobbly belly.
A very scary
Babbling blob.
An oversized quivering
Doorknob.
A swamp of blancmange,
A circle gone wrong,
A marauding monster
With gobbly jaws.
The bulldog next door;
Horrace, the Human Dough;
The Thing from Goodness Only Knows.

Oh ol' jellyfish face
Was a favorite with the kids
For all the contortions
And impressions he did.

Frightening them completely
Out of their minds,

So loving and so kind.

MARSHMALLOW, POOR FELLOW

The marshmallow's life
Is a pitiful one
And also not very long.
It grows, as you know,
Down there in the marsh
Where conditions aren't mellow but harsh.
In fact, they are quite atrocious,
For it's immediately picked
By small children with sticks
And taken away and roasted.

WHAT THE LITTLE BRICK BUILT

The little brick didn't like it,
Really didn't like it at all.
There it was stranded and stuck,
Stuck in the middle of a wall.

It wasn't so much the wall,
It was the dreariness of the design.
Big and broad and bland,
But perhaps a sign of the times.

And so a decision was made—
It would simply run away.
Leave all its bricky buddies,
And a gaping hole, I'm afraid.

And down the road it ran,
A road without end in sight.
But a brick without a wall—
What was the meaning of life?

Yet as fate often transpires,
It found that it was not alone,
And there were many similar bricks
Wallless and far from home.

Bricks unlike your basic brick
(Boring and brittle and thick),
But bricks, bright and bohemian—
Independent, bricks that could think!

That wanted to change the world,
That could not conform to a wall
Or sit all silent and complacent,
But had blueprints of dreams and more.

Designs they were intimately part of.
Designs unique and inspired.
Architectural enlightenment and wonder,
Elegant arches and towering spires.

Bricks that would build their own dreams,
That saw a fabulous future ahead—
Humble houses and vast cities
Imagined anew in their heads.

And from such vivid visions,
From these small rebellious roots,
Come the Great Achievements—
The blossom and the fruit.

And far, far over that distant horizon,
Far, far down that winding road,
The little brick went and built its dreams—
A brand new beauty to behold.

SPACE POODLES

These cute little alien dogs
(New from outer space),
Won't fetch a stick,
Won't sit and beg,
Won't lovingly lick your face.
Won't bring your slippers,
Won't come when called,
Won't go for walkies in the park.
Won't do any of that doggy stuff at all.
But still there's one thing you can't ignore—
They make wonderful watchdogs for sure.

WHERE ARE THEY NOW?
(An Invisible Family Portrait)

The Invisible Man has a brother
Though they see very little of each other.

He also has a sister, ol' See-Through Sue,
But where she is now, he hasn't a clue.

As for his invisible mom and dad,
I'm afraid the story is a little bit sad.

For he's never seen head nor hair of the pair.
It's as if they've never been there.

O Invisible Man, I'm glad I'm not you.
For although all your family may perhaps be at home,
I'd hate to be standing in your invisible shoes.
You might as well be living completely alone.

THE GREAT ESCAPIST

A man of worldly fame,
His reputation, his name, were made
By escaping from a paper bag in the rain
Tied up with daisy chains.
He could escape from an unlocked room
In about three minutes flat,
Though amazing as it seems,
It's hard to believe that fact.

Yet this I know is true—
An act not easily forgotten—
The time he escaped from a old shoe box
Bound up with sewing cotton.
How did he go and do it?
No one really knows.
But of course he could bend
Bare bars with his toes
And pick a lock with the end of his nose.

ONCE (AND THAT'S QUITE ENOUGH)

There once was an old bald man
Who on his head, a hare he'd wear.
And although up there was completely bare,
He always said he had a little hare.

There once was a flying carpet
That flew off with a large armchair,
Leaving behind the comfy sofa.
That's when life just doesn't seem fair.

There once was an amorous cow
Who eloped with a lush green field.
Whether it was love or lush,
She was never at a loss for a meal.

There once was a very beginning
That met up with nearly the end,
Then off they ran down Runaway Road
And are down there . . .

175

. . . round the bend.

(Just like Uncle Mozz, my friends.)

INDEX OF TITLES

INDEX OF FIRST LINES

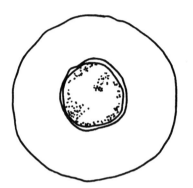

TO CONTACT ME

Please ring this bell,
And if you get no answer, friend,
In a short while, ring it again.
And wait a few minutes, or, better, a few days.
Then try it again, I'd say.
(Sometimes there's a loose connection,
The wires are frayed.)
But if still you get no answer, no response,
Then slam the book shut (for luck)
And hurl it heartily at the wall (at least once).
Then pick it up (be a bit rough)
And get out the garden hose.
(Or you can phone for a fire truck, I suppose.)
And thoroughly saturate and soak it,
Then open up a tub of treacle and coat it,
Before you shake it and take it
And pop it in the oven and bake it.
(For no less than sixty-six days. That should do it, I'd say.)
Then bring it out, perhaps bash it about
(Remembering to wear your oven gloves),
And give it to a passing turtle dove
Who can then take it miles up into the sky
And drop it down from up there so high
That it lands with a great big almighty THUMP!
All mangled and mutilated in a messy ol' lump.
Then open it carefully. (Okay, shake it a few more times!)
And try the bell again—it should work fine.

SO LONG—
BUT YOU'VE STILL NOT GONE

And so you said goodbye,
And skipped down the garden path.
And waved, with a little laugh,
Saying, "Oh dear, it's so very late,"
As you reached the garden gate.
And you waved as you started down the road,
And I waved back with my handkerchief so,
Feeling somewhat sad and somewhat alone.
And you waved again when you reached the trees,
And again by the rolling fields.
And you waved by the waves
Of the salty green sea,
And still your little hand I could see.
And as you started up the far-off hill,
I could see you there waving still.
And as the sun sank slowly in the sky,
Why, there you were, waving goodbye.

You said, "So long. I'll see you later."
And it's later and later and later,
And still you wave,
And still I stay,
Waving, waving, waving.
(Now it's started raining.)
And though I'm not one for complaining,
Sometimes I really wonder why
You ever bothered to say goodbye.

UNCLE ED'S HEAD